Death
and
Dying

Opposing Viewpoints®

James Haley, *Book Editor*

Daniel Leone, *President*
Bonnie Szumski, *Publisher*
Scott Barbour, *Managing Editor*
Helen Cothran, *Senior Editor*

GREENHAVEN
PRESS®

THOMSON
™
GALE

San Diego • Detroit • New York • San Francisco • Cleveland
New Haven, Conn. • Waterville, Maine • London • Munich

For more information, contact
Greenhaven Press
27500 Drake Rd.
Farmington Hills, MI 48331-3535
Or you can visit our Internet site at http://www.gale.com

Cover credit: © Eyewire

LIBRARY OF CONGRESS CATALOGING-IN-PUBLICATION DATA

Death and dying / James Haley, book editor.
    p. cm. — (Opposing viewpoints series)
    Includes bibliographical references and index.
    ISBN 0-7377-1223-6 (pbk. : alk. paper) — ISBN 0-7377-1224-4 (cloth : alk. paper)
    1. Death. 2. Terminal care. 3. Euthanasia. 4. Assisted suicide. I. Haley, James, 1968– . II. Series.
R726.8 .D376 2003
306.9—dc21
                                             2002072223

"Congress shall make no law. . . abridging the freedom of speech, or of the press."

First Amendment to the U.S. Constitution

The basic foundation of our democracy is the First Amendment guarantee of freedom of expression. The Opposing Viewpoints Series is dedicated to the concept of this basic freedom and the idea that it is more important to practice it than to enshrine it.

Contents

Why Consider Opposing Viewpoints?

"The only way in which a human being can make some approach to knowing the whole of a subject is by hearing what can be said about it by persons of every variety of opinion and studying all modes in which it can be looked at by every character of mind. No wise man ever acquired his wisdom in any mode but this."

John Stuart Mill

In our media-intensive culture it is not difficult to find differing opinions. Thousands of newspapers and magazines and dozens of radio and television talk shows resound with differing points of view. The difficulty lies in deciding which opinion to agree with and which "experts" seem the most credible. The more inundated we become with differing opinions and claims, the more essential it is to hone critical reading and thinking skills to evaluate these ideas. Opposing Viewpoints books address this problem directly by presenting stimulating debates that can be used to enhance and teach these skills. The varied opinions contained in each book examine many different aspects of a single issue. While examining these conveniently edited opposing views, readers can develop critical thinking skills such as the ability to compare and contrast authors' credibility, facts, argumentation styles, use of persuasive techniques, and other stylistic tools. In short, the Opposing Viewpoints Series is an ideal way to attain the higher-level thinking and reading skills so essential in a culture of diverse and contradictory opinions.

In addition to providing a tool for critical thinking, Opposing Viewpoints books challenge readers to question their own strongly held opinions and assumptions. Most people form their opinions on the basis of upbringing, peer pressure, and personal, cultural, or professional bias. By reading carefully balanced opposing views, readers must directly confront new ideas as well as the opinions of those with whom they disagree. This is not to simplistically argue that everyone who reads opposing views will—or should—change his or her opinion. Instead, the series enhances readers' understanding of their own views by encouraging confrontation with opposing ideas. Careful examination of others' views can lead to the readers' understanding of the logical inconsistencies in their own opinions, perspective on why they hold an opinion, and the consideration of the possibility that their opinion requires further evaluation.

Evaluating Other Opinions

To ensure that this type of examination occurs, Opposing Viewpoints books present all types of opinions. Prominent spokespeople on different sides of each issue as well as well-known professionals from many disciplines challenge the reader. An additional goal of the series is to provide a forum for other, less known, or even unpopular viewpoints. The opinion of an ordinary person who has had to make the decision to cut off life support from a terminally ill relative, for example, may be just as valuable and provide just as much insight as a medical ethicist's professional opinion. The editors have two additional purposes in including these less known views. One, the editors encourage readers to respect others' opinions—even when not enhanced by professional credibility. It is only by reading or listening to and objectively evaluating others' ideas that one can determine whether they are worthy of consideration. Two, the inclusion of such viewpoints encourages the important critical thinking skill of objectively evaluating an author's credentials and bias. This evaluation will illuminate an author's reasons for taking a particular stance on an issue and will aid in readers' evaluation of the author's ideas.

It is our hope that these books will give readers a deeper understanding of the issues debated and an appreciation of the complexity of even seemingly simple issues when good and honest people disagree. This awareness is particularly important in a democratic society such as ours in which people enter into public debate to determine the common good. Those with whom one disagrees should not be regarded as enemies but rather as people whose views deserve careful examination and may shed light on one's own.

Thomas Jefferson once said that "difference of opinion leads to inquiry, and inquiry to truth." Jefferson, a broadly educated man, argued that "if a nation expects to be ignorant and free . . . it expects what never was and never will be." As individuals and as a nation, it is imperative that we consider the opinions of others and examine them with skill and discernment. The Opposing Viewpoints Series is intended to help readers achieve this goal.

David L. Bender and Bruno Leone,
Founders

Greenhaven Press anthologies primarily consist of previously published material taken from a variety of sources, including periodicals, books, scholarly journals, newspapers, government documents, and position papers from private and public organizations. These original sources are often edited for length and to ensure their accessibility for a young adult audience. The anthology editors also change the original titles of these works in order to clearly present the main thesis of each viewpoint and to explicitly indicate the opinion presented in the viewpoint. These alterations are made in consideration of both the reading and comprehension levels of a young adult audience. Every effort is made to ensure that Greenhaven Press accurately reflects the original intent of the authors included in this anthology.

Introduction

"Strive though we may to ignore or postpone our date with death, sooner or later it comes."
—Michael M. Uhlmann, "How Do We Die?" World & I, 1998.

Scientific advances notwithstanding, one feature of human existence remains constant—life inexorably leads to death. Whether it is the death of a loved one, the onset of a terminal illness, or reaching the limits of a natural life span, at some point in a person's life he or she will be confronted by the medical, spiritual, and ethical issues that death encompasses. A person can choose to utterly ignore death, tirelessly dwell on it, or find a middle ground, but eventually, life, at least on this plane of existence, will come to an end.

Because it is so closely linked to a society's religious and social mores, the process of death and dying is viewed quite differently in cultures around the world. Asian, Middle Eastern, and European countries approach the at-once natural and utterly mysterious persistence of death in unique ways. In Japan, for example, the parents of aborted fetuses hold memorial ceremonies in Buddhist temples for their "water child." The dead child's name is written on a stick and placed in a temple stream, symbolizing the child's "suspended state in a stream of rebirth," according to Lawrence E. Sullivan, director of the Harvard University Center for the Study of World Religions. In the Netherlands, Dutch doctors have shown a willingness to assist in the deaths of patients who are not terminally ill but simply wish to end their lives. In April 2001, the parliament in the Netherlands passed legislation making euthanasia completely legal, granting doctors the right to end the lives of patients who are in excessive pain—or who simply decide that life is no longer worth living. This tolerance for physician-assisted suicide stands in stark contrast to cultural attitudes prevalent in the United States, where the right-to-die activist Jack Kervorkian is serving a lengthy prison term for assisting in the deaths of mostly terminally ill patients.

Some observers maintain that Americans are in a state of denial when it comes to matters related to death and dying. American culture places a premium on material success and tends to turn away from more contemplative, spiritual matters. Explains Dana G. Cable, a professor of psychology at Hood College in Frederick, Maryland, "Most other cultures see death as part of the whole life experience, but in our country, we hide behind terminology. We 'go to our eternal rest,' we 'expire' instead of die in the hospital and in funeral homes, you are put in the 'slumber room.' We say people 'pass away' instead of die. We have 'memorial services' for them. All this language avoids facing the reality of the truth."

Over the past fifty years, rapid advances in health and medicine have deepened the resistance of many Americans toward accepting death as a natural fact of life. According to physician Robert Buckman, experimental drugs, organ transplants, and other medical advances plant "in the back of our minds" the perception that death "can be prevented forever with just another little bit of technical know-how. . . . And as our expectations of a healthy life increase, the thought of dying seems ever more alien and unnatural." Death has become an event to be mastered by technology; another triumph of the American can-do spirit.

Increasingly, however, a growing movement of physicians, psychologists, social workers, and others, has begun to question whether Americans should expend so much energy in attempting to postpone and control death. The publication of Elisabeth Kubler-Ross's book *On Death and Dying* in 1969 is credited with the birth of this "death awareness" movement. According to Donald Heinz in his book *The Last Passage: Recovering a Death of Our Own*, Kubler-Ross concluded that the dying person typically moves through five stages, from denial to anger to bargaining to depression to acceptance. Acceptance, and the potential for growth associated with it, became a well-known goal, which Kubler-Ross thought appropriate for every dying patient. She began calling for "the rejection of a lonely, mechanical, dehumanized environment for the dying. . . . In this way, humans could develop a proper response to the dying and to their own mortality."

One result of Kubler-Ross's work has been a reexamination

of the role of medical technology in the treatment of the terminally ill. To Kubler-Ross and her supporters, the dying process offers a chance for spiritual and emotional growth that is too often overshadowed by dubious medical intervention. Some health care professionals have come to share her view that the over-use of life-support machines does a disservice to the terminally ill by causing unnecessary, drawn-out suffering. They claim that the final months of a dying patient's life could be better spent coming to terms with life's end and saying goodbye to friends and loved ones in a warm caring environment, preferably within the patient's own home.

A philosophy of treatment for the terminally ill known as "hospice care" was pioneered by British physician Cicely Saunders in the late 1960s, roughly coinciding with the emergence of Kubler-Ross's book and the death awareness movement. Explains Peter G. Filene in his book *In the Arms of Others: A Cultural History of the Right-to-Die in America*, "In 1967, Dr. Cicely Saunders established St. Christopher's [hospice] . . . in order to help people travel contentedly through the last stage of their lives. She surrounded them with the feel of home and family—a caring community. More fundamentally her staff—doctors, nurses, social workers, chaplain, volunteers—did not fight against terminal disease but helped people live with it. Healing acquired a different meaning. 'Sometimes healing means . . . finding new wholeness as a family—being reconciled,' Saunders said. 'Or it can mean easing the pain of dying or allowing someone to die when the time comes.' In the words of the hospice slogan: Neither hasten nor prolong death."

Over the past several decades, the hospice movement has evolved into an important treatment option for the terminally ill. Death awareness proponents contend that hospice care is much more meaningful to dying patients, whose comfort is put before life-prolonging treatments. Most hospice patients are cared for in their own homes by a diverse staff based on Saunders's model. The numbers of dying patients who elect hospice care remains small—the vast majority of people still die in nursing homes and hospitals—but those who have been involved in the movement contend that hospice care has helped countless people deal positively with death by making it more visible and natural to the patient's friends and family.

Hospice care is one example of how some Americans are reflecting on what death means to the dying, their family members, and the greater culture. Hospice care is a small movement but may be indicative of a larger need to come to terms with death as individuals and as a society. In addition to improving the care of the terminally ill, other examples of how people are seeking a new approach to death and dying include developing better ways to cope with grief, extending the human life span, and investigating life after death. The authors in *Death and Dying: Opposing Viewpoints* discuss these issues in the following chapters: How Should End-of-Life Care Be Improved? How Can People Cope with Death? Should Effort to Expand the Human Life Span Be Pursued? Is There Life After Death? To be sure the issues surrounding death and dying affect everyone, for, as Shakespeare wrote, "Death, a necessary end, will come when it will come."

CHAPTER 1

How Should End-of-Life Care Be Improved?

Chapter Preface

In the fall of 1975, the country was captivated by the fate of Karen Ann Quinlan, a New Jersey woman who had lapsed into a coma months earlier after a night of drug use. Karen was being kept alive by a respirator machine and had only a slim chance for revival, but her doctors denied the Quinlans' wishes that she be allowed to die. In response, her parents filed suit in New Jersey state court to have her removed from life support. In March 1976, the New Jersey Supreme Court delivered the landmark ruling that Karen's parents were qualified to exercise her "right to die" while she remained irreversibly incapacitated.

Quinlan's physicians, however, had a different interpretation of what removing Quinlan from life support entailed. They gradually "weaned" Karen off life support by intermittently removing the respirator and restoring it as soon as Karen struggled to breathe. Eventually, while Karen remained in a persistent vegetative state, she was able to breathe on her own. Her parents had no choice but to transfer her to a nursing home where she remained until her death in 1985.

The highly publicized trial and Karen's drawn-out death raised public concern about the downside of aggressive end-of-life treatment that too often ignores the wishes of patients and their families. Explains Peter G. Filene in the book *In the Arms of Others: A Cultural History of the Right-to-Die in America*, "Modern medicine produced modern dying: a prolonged process rather than a distinct event, which thereby made the very definition of death ambiguous and subjective." In addition, according to Dr. William Knaus, a critical care specialist, "There is a tragic mismatch between the health care many seriously ill and dying people want and what they get."

To prevent the loss of control and sense of ambiguity surrounding end-of-life care, many people have taken to preparing advance directives—legal documents that instruct doctors and family members what measures should or should not be taken once a person becomes incapacitated by an illness. The "living will" is a type of advance directive that a person can draw up prior to becoming ill and use to specifically state whether they wish to be kept alive on life support. The durable power of attorney for health care is another commonly used type of advance directive. It allows a person to appoint a health care proxy to make decisions for them. Randall K. Hanson, a professor of business law at the University of North Carolina warns that "without written directives in many states, it is very difficult, time consuming, expensive, and emotionally devastating to cease life support procedures."

However, some observers caution that advance directives do not give people as much control over their treatment as they would like to believe. Many living wills, for example, cannot adequately account for the circumstances of an unforeseen illness. Contends University of Michigan law professor Carl E. Schneider, "People preparing advance directives . . . face the special problems of making decisions for a hypothetical future. They must imagine what they would want at an unspecifiable time stricken with an unidentifiable illness with unpredictable treatments."

As the Karen Ann Quinlan case dramatically illustrates, end-of-life treatment is fraught with complex legal and ethical issues that are further complicated once a patient loses the ability to communicate his or her wishes. Advance directives are one method that people are employing to enhance their end-of-life care. The viewpoints in the following chapter debate and explore other ways that end-of-life care should be improved.

> *"[Hospice] help[s] the terminally ill live as fully as possible until they die."*

Hospice Care Improves End-of-Life Care

Joe Loconte

Hospice is a concept of care for terminally ill patients that emphasizes pain management and comfort over medical efforts to prolong life. Those near death are usually treated in their own homes by doctors, nurses, social workers, volunteer aides, and family members. In the following viewpoint, Joe Loconte maintains that hospice care is an important option for patients who do not wish to die a depersonalized death in a hospital or attempt assisted suicide. According to Loconte, the hospice philosophy is about reducing pain, which routinely goes undertreated in hospitals. In addition, hospice enables the terminally ill to face death in a more spiritual and emotionally supportive setting. The author is the deputy editor of *Policy Review: The Journal of American Citizenship*, a bimonthly magazine.

As you read, consider the following questions:
1. Why have most terminally ill patients never heard about the hospice option, in the author's opinion?
2. According to Loconte, who is credited with founding the modern hospice movement?
3. How does the case of terminally ill patient John Brown illustrate the benefits of pain management practiced by hospice teams?

In the deepening debate over assisted suicide, almost everyone agrees on a few troubling facts: Most people with terminal illnesses die in the sterile settings of hospitals or nursing homes, often in prolonged, uncontrolled pain; physicians typically fail to manage their patients' symptoms, adding mightily to their suffering; the wishes of patients are ignored as they are subjected to intrusive, often futile, medical interventions; and aggressive end-of-life care often bankrupts families that are already in crisis.

Too many people in America are dying a bad death.

The solution, some tell us, is physician-assisted suicide. Oregon has legalized the practice for the terminally ill. Michigan's Jack Kevorkian continues to help willing patients end their own lives [Kevorkian is serving a ten to twenty-five year prison sentence for second-degree murder.] The prestigious *New England Journal of Medicine* has come out in favor of doctor-assisted death. Says Faye Girsh, the director of the Hemlock Society: "The only way to achieve a quick and painless and certain death is through medications that only a physician has access to."

Hospice: A More Dignified Death

This, we are told, is death with dignity. What we do not often hear is that there is another way to die—under the care of a specialized discipline of medicine that manages the pain of deadly diseases, keeps patients comfortable yet awake and alert, and surrounds the dying with emotional and spiritual support. Every year, roughly 450,000 people die in this way. They die in hospice.

"The vast majority of terminally ill patients can have freedom from pain and clarity of mind," says Martha Twaddle, a leading hospice physician and medical director at the hospice division of the Palliative CareCenter of the North Shore, in Evanston, Illinois. "Hospice care helps liberate patients from the afflictions of their symptoms so that they can truly live until they die."

The hospice concept rejects decisions to hasten death, but also extreme medical efforts to prolong life for the terminally ill. Rather, it aggressively treats the symptoms of disease—pain, fatigue, disorientation, depression—to ease the emotional suffering of those near death. It applies "palliative medicine," a team-based philosophy of caregiving that unites the medical know-how of doctors and nurses with the practical and emotional support of social workers, volunteer aides, and spiritual counselors. Because the goal of hospice is comfort, not cure, patients are usually treated at home, where most say they would prefer to die.

"Most people nowadays see two options: A mechanized, depersonalized, and painful death in a hospital or a swift death that rejects medical institutions and technology," says Nicholas Christakis, an assistant professor of medicine and sociology at the University of Chicago. "It is a false choice. Hospice offers a way out of this dilemma."

Hospice or Hemlock?

If so, there remains a gauntlet of cultural roadblocks. Hospice is rarely mentioned in medical school curricula. Says Dale Smith, a former head of the American Academy of Hospice and Palliative Medicine, "Talk to any physician and he'll tell you he never got any training in ways to deal with patients at the end of life."

The result: Most terminally ill patients either never hear about the hospice option or enter a program on the brink of death. Though a recent Gallup Poll shows that nine out of 10 Americans would choose to die at home once they are diagnosed with a terminal disease, most spend their final days in hospitals or nursing homes.

And, too often, that's not a very good place to die. A four-year research project funded by the Robert Wood Johnson Foundation looked at more than 9,000 seriously ill patients in five major teaching hospitals. Considered one of the most important studies on medical care for the dying, it found that doctors routinely subject patients to futile treatment, ignore their specific instructions for care, and allow them to die in needless pain.

"We are failing in our responsibility to provide humane care for people who are dying," says Ira Byock, a leading hospice physician and the author of *Dying Well*. George Annas, the director of the Law, Medicine and Ethics Program at Boston University, puts it even more starkly: "If dying patients want to retain some control over their dying process, they must get out of the hospital."

That's precisely the argument that hospice advocates have been making for the last 25 years. Hospice programs are, in fact, the only institution in the country with a record of compassionate, end-of-life care for people with incurable illnesses. The hospice movement, and the palliative approach to medicine it represents, could revolutionize America's culture of dying.

Since the mid-1970s, hospice programs have grown from a mere handful to more than 2,500, available in nearly every community. At least 4,000 nurses are now nationally certified in hospice techniques. In Michigan—Kevorkian's home state—a statewide hospice program cares for 1,100 people a day, regardless of their ability to pay. The Robert Wood Johnson Foundation, a leading health-care philanthropy, has launched a $12-million initiative to improve care for the dying. And the American Medical Association, which did not even recognize hospice as a medical discipline until 1995, has made the training of physicians in end-of-life care one of its top priorities.

There is a conflict raging in America today over society's obligations to care for its most vulnerable. Says Charles von Gunten, a hospice specialist at Northwestern Memorial Hospital, in Chicago, "It is fundamentally an argument about the soul of medicine." One observer calls it a choice between hospice or hemlock—between a compassion that "suffers with" the dying, or one that eliminates suffering by eliminating the sufferer.

A New Vision of Medicine

The modern hospice movement was founded by English physician Cicely Saunders, who, as a nurse in a London clinic, was aghast at the disregard for the emotional and spiritual suffering of patients near death. In 1967, she opened St. Christopher's Hospice, an in-patient facility drawing on spiritual and practical support from local congregations.

"She wanted to introduce a distinctly Christian vision to mainstream medicine," says Nigel Cameron, an expert in bioethics at Trinity International University, in Deerfield, Illinois. The staples of the hospice philosophy quickly emerged: at-home care; an interdisciplinary team of physicians, nurses, pharmacists, ministers, and social workers; and a heavy sprinkling of volunteers.

Saunders's vision got a boost from *On Death and Dying*, Elizabeth Kubler-Ross's book based on more than 500 interviews with dying patients. The study, in which the author pleaded for greater attention to the psychosocial aspects of dying, became an international bestseller. By 1974, the National Cancer Institute had begun funding hospices; the first, in Branford, Connecticut, was regarded as a national model of home care for the terminally ill.

A Familial Model of Care

Hospice works as much with a patient's family as with the patient herself, for terminal illness inescapably involves them too. They have to move her bedroom downstairs and install a hospital bed. They have to take up the housework, cooking, child care, or yard work that she used to do. They need to learn which pills are for which symptoms and how to adjust a breathing tube. They must husband the stamina to carry on through the next weeks or months, no one knows how long. To assist with these multiple problems, hospice staff includes doctors, nurses, social workers, chaplains, and volunteers—a health-care team that incorporates the family as another member. The experience of dying extends beyond the dying person and even beyond her death. "Don't forget," said the director of the New Haven hospice, "that the family lives on after the patient." And so most hospice programs organize bereavement classes or support groups.

Peter G. Filene, *In the Arms of Others*, 1998.

Early hospice programs were independent and community-run, managed by local physicians or registered nurses. Most operated on a shoestring, relying on contributions, patient payments, and private insurance. Many were relatively spartan, consisting of little more than a nurse and a social worker making home visits.

Religious communities were early and natural supporters. "The questions people ask at the end of life are religious questions," says Rabbi Maurice Lamm, the president of the

National Institute for Jewish Hospice, "and they must be answered by somebody who knows the person's faith." Synagogues, which usually support visitation committees for the sick, formed commissions to establish a Jewish presence in hospitals offering hospice care. The Catholic Church took a leadership role: Through its hospitals, health-care systems, and parishes, it began providing hospice beds, nurses, and priests.

By the mid-1980s, the movement started to take off. As hospital costs escalated, Medicare joined a growing number of insurance companies that offered reimbursement for hospice's home-care approach. In 1985, President Ronald Reagan signed legislation making the Medicare hospice benefit a permanent part of the Medicare program.

Today nearly 80 percent of hospices qualify. Medicare picks up most of the bill for services, from pain medications to special beds. The majority of managed-care plans offer at least partial coverage, and most private insurance plans include a hospice benefit. Since becoming a part of Medicare, hospice has seen a four-fold increase in patients receiving its services.

Redefining Autonomy

The starting place for any hospice team is the patient: What kind of care does he or she really want? "It's not about our goals for a patient," says Dorothy Pitner, the president of the Palliative CareCenter of the North Shore, which cares for about 200 people a day in Chicago's northern suburbs. "They tell us how they define quality of life, and then together we decide the course of action."

This is how hospice respects patient autonomy: not by hastening death, but by working closely with patients and families to weigh the costs and benefits of care. "Patients have the right to refuse unwanted, futile medical care," says Walter Hunter, the chairman of the National Hospice Ethics Committee. "But the right to refuse care does not mean the right to demand active assistance in dying." Patients resolve the tradeoffs between controlling pain and feeling alert; they choose whether to use a medical device that provides them with nutrients but causes swelling and congestion.

Though physicians and medical directors may make only a few visits to a patient's home over the course of an illness, they supervise all caregiving decisions by the hospice teams. No one fills a prescription, inserts a tube, or gives medication without their OK. The central task of getting a person's pain under control falls to doctors, working closely with pharmacists.

Registered nurses serve as case managers. Usually they are the first to enter the home of the dying, make an assessment, and describe symptoms to physicians. They visit the home weekly and are on call 24 hours a day for emergencies. Nurses, along with nurse's aides, not only act as the go-between for families and physicians; they also bear much of the burden for making sure patients are comfortable, from administering drugs to drawing blood to suggesting medications or therapies. Says Marty Ayers, the executive director of the Hospice and Palliative Nurses Association, "The nurses are still breaking ground on what works for people."

Volunteers are also important to that work. For several hours a week they help out at home, cooking or doing household chores, keeping an eye on bed-ridden patients, or just listening as family members struggle with grief. Last year, about 100,000 volunteers joined 30,000 paid staff in hospices nationwide. They are, as one veteran caregiver puts it, the "sponges" in the mix, soaking up some of the anguish that accompanies death and dying.

The Death Wish

Hospice care usually begins where traditional medicine ends: when it becomes clear that a person's illness will not succumb to even the most heroic of medical therapies. "This is the toughest problem for doctors and families, the issue of letting go," says Alan Smookler, the Palliative CareCenter's assistant medical director. "There's a lot of technology out there—feeding tubes, antibiotics, oxygen, ventilators, dialysis—and the hardest problem is saying that these interventions are no longer beneficial."

Such was the case for John Brown, diagnosed with terminal cancer. Brown (not his real name) was treated with radiation and chemotherapy in a Washington, D.C.–area hospital. The treatments proved ineffective, and the pain from his cancer got worse. His wife convinced him to enter care at a local hospice program.

"His immediate request was that his wife call several friends, all of whom were hunters, and ask them to shoot him," says the Reverend Jeanne Brenneis, of the Hospice of Northern Virginia. "This was a man very used to being in control, and he was frightened of being helpless and in pain."

The hospice team concentrated first on relieving Brown's physical discomfort. His physician prescribed several pain-killing drugs, while a nurse watched for other symptoms. Within a couple of days, his pain was under control.

Though mostly bed-bound, Brown spent the next five months at home laboring as best he could at his favorite hobby: boat design. The hospice team set up a drafting board by his bedside so he could go on working. He finished one design and was halfway through another when he died.

He caught up on some other business as well: spending time with his wife and adult daughters and, after years of avoiding church, coming to terms with God. "He had time to reflect and think," Brenneis says, "and he grew a great deal emotionally and spiritually in that time."

Losing Control

Brown's story is no longer remarkable. Interviews with hospice caregivers uncover a singular experience: Once the pain and symptoms of an illness are under control, people rarely talk about taking their own lives. "Those requests go away with good palliative care," says von Gunten, who directs palliative education at Northwestern University Medical School. "I see this on a routine basis." . . .

By interrupting sleep, curbing appetite, and discouraging personal interactions, pain doesn't just aggravate a person's physical condition. It also leads, as a recent report by the Institute of Medicine puts it, to "depression and demoralization" of the sufferer. Says David English, the president of the Hospice of Northern Virginia, one of the nation's oldest programs, "You can't address the psychosocial issues of a person who is in pain."

Hospice has understood this connection between pain

and overall well-being from the start. After conventional treatments fail, says Martha Twaddle, "you'll often hear doctors say 'there's nothing left to do.' There's a lot left to do. There is a lot of aggressive care that can be given to you to treat your symptoms."

Hardly anyone doubts that more energetic caregiving for the dying is in order. A 1990 report from the National Cancer Institute warned that "undertreatment of pain and other symptoms of cancer is a serious and neglected public health problem." The New York State Task Force on Life and the Law, in arguing against legalizing assisted suicide, cited the "pervasive failure of our health-care system to treat pain and diagnose and treat depression."

The best studies show that most doctors still undertreat pain and that most people with chronic and terminal illnesses experience needless suffering. A survey was taken a few years ago of 1,177 U.S. physicians who had cared for more than 70,000 patients with cancer during the previous six months. Eighty-five percent said the majority of cancer patients with pain were undermedicated; nearly half of those surveyed rated their own pain management techniques as fair or very poor. . . .

A Debt to Hospice

The pain-control approach of hospice depends on an aggressive use of opioid drugs—narcotics such as morphine, fentanyl, codeine, or methadone. Despite the effectiveness of these drugs in clinical settings, euthanasia supporters often ignore or contest the results. Timothy Quill, a leading advocate of doctor-assisted suicide, writes that "there is no empirical evidence that all physical suffering associated with incurable illness can be effectively relieved."

Ira Byock, the president of the American Academy of Hospice and Palliative Medicine, says that's medical bunk. A 20-year hospice physician, Byock has cared for thousands of patients with terminal disease. "The best hospice and palliative-care programs have demonstrated that pain and physical suffering can always be alleviated," he says. "Not necessarily eliminated, but it can always be lessened and made more tolerable.". . .

Though most of the pain management research conducted over the last decade has occurred in academic and clinical settings, the front-line work of hospice staff has added significantly to what we know about mitigating pain and suffering. Says Cleary: "Hospice has been a part of the whole learning process because they care for cancer patients, and most of what we've learned has come from them." Patricia Berry, of the Wisconsin Cancer Pain Initiative, goes a step further: "The hospice movement finally legitimized the practice of pain management.". . .

The Road Ahead

What started out as something of a revolt against traditional medicine is slowly becoming mainstream. In important ways, hospice remains faithful to Saunders's vision of comprehensive, home-based care to the terminally ill. In 1997, at least three-quarters of hospice patients died at home. Though most of its clients suffer from cancer, hospice now treats those with a range of life-threatening diseases, including Alzheimer's, lung disease, heart disease, and AIDS.

Despite the growing reach of hospice, however, too many people still enter a program already at death's doorstep. Says Naomi Naierman, the president of the American Hospice Foundation, "The resistance on the part of physicians to introduce hospice before the brink of death is a major barrier." According to one study, the median length of survival after entering hospice is barely two months. More than one in four patients dies within two weeks, many within a couple of days. Researchers from the University of Chicago and the University of Pennsylvania concluded in a 1996 report that "most hospice patients enter the programs too late to benefit from them."

Moreover, the mainstreaming of hospice is posing new challenges. Medicare funding has made its rapid growth possible and helped professionalize its services. But it also has institutionalized the movement, making it less connected to community support and much more dependent on government funding.

Only about 28 percent of all hospices are now independent and community-based; nearly half are operated by hospitals or home health agencies. In its early years, hospice ran primarily on grants, charitable donations, and volunteers. Medicare now pays for about two-thirds of all hospice care. For-profit hospices, spurred on by the availability of Medicare, constitute 15 percent of the industry. Observers say avoiding the worst excesses of managed care may be one of the movement's greatest challenges. . . .

Living Until They Die

Even the goal of easing people's suffering, as central as it is to hospice care, is not an end in itself. The aim of comfort is part of a larger objective: to help the terminally ill live as fully as possible until they die. This is where hospice departs most pointedly both from traditional medicine and the advocates of assisted suicide.

Hospice, by shining a light on the emotional and spiritual aspects of suffering, is challenging the medical community to re-examine its priorities. The period at the end of life, simultaneously ignored and micromanaged by conventional approaches, can be filled with significance. To neglect it is to diminish ourselves. "Spiritual inattentiveness in the face of dying and death can lead to the sad spectacle of medical technology run amok," says Laurence O'Connell, the president of the Park Ridge Center, a medical ethics think tank in Chicago. . . .

Hospice or hemlock: Though both end in death, each pursues its vision of a "good death" along radically different paths. At its deepest level, the hospice philosophy strikes a blow at the notion of the isolated individual. It insists that no one dies in a vacuum. Where one exists, hospice physicians, nurses, and social workers rush in to help fill it.

*"Hospice care depend[s] on a highly
questionable ideology that . . . can be . . .
reasonably rejected by many [terminally ill
patients]."*

Hospice Care Is Not Appropriate for All Terminally Ill Patients

Felicia Ackerman

In the following viewpoint, Felicia Ackerman argues that hospice care, a concept of care for the terminally ill that places patient comfort and family needs before medical efforts to prolong life, is based on questionable principles that should be rejected by most patients. Hospice care abdicates medicine's primary responsibility to put the patient first by diverting attention from patient to family, in the author's opinion. In addition, expecting the terminally ill to serenely accept death as "natural" requires them to have a sacrificial view of their lives. Ackerman is a professor of philosophy at Brown University.

As you read, consider the following questions:

1. In the author's opinion, how does the religious aspect of the hospice movement impair its ability to care for nonreligious people?
2. Why should hospice care allow each patient to decide for herself whether the possible discomfort of medical treatment is worth the prolonged life, according to Ackerman?
3. In Ackerman's opinion, how does involving families and loved ones in patient care sacrifice the interests of the patient?

Excerpted from "Goldilocks and Mrs. Ilych: A Critical Look at the 'Philosophy of Hospice,'" by Felicia Ackerman, *Cambridge Quarterly of Healthcare Ethics*, Summer 1997. Copyright © 1997 by Cambridge University Press. Reprinted with permission.

Anyone who thinks contemporary American society is hopelessly contentious and lacking in shared values has probably not been paying attention to the way the popular media portray the hospice movement. Over and over, we are told such things as that "Humane care costs less than high-tech care and is what patients want and need," that hospices are "the most effective and least expensive route to a dignified death," that hospice personnel are "heroic," that their "compassion and dedication seem inexhaustible," and that "few could argue with the powerful message that it is better [for dying patients] to leave wrapped in the love of family and care givers than locked in the cold, metallic embrace of a machine."

Escaping Scrutiny

Few do argue with this message. Even in professional circles, hospices seem largely to escape the sort of critical scrutiny that society routinely gives to business, government, and the schools. This viewpoint aims to remedy that lack. I will focus on analyzing and criticizing the principles of hospice care, although there will be some discussion of hospices in actual practice as well, especially insofar as the practices help clarify what the principles really amount to. I will argue that several principles of hospice care depend on a highly questionable ideology that, while valuable to some terminally ill people, can be (and apparently is) reasonably rejected by many others. This argument has major implications for health policy, as it militates against any public policy that would favor hospice care over other types of care for the dying.

The following principles constitute the National Hospice Organization's "Philosophy of Hospice."

1. Hospice implies acceptance of death as a natural part of the life cycle.
2. When death is inevitable, hospice will neither seek to hasten it nor to postpone it.
3. Patients, their families and loved ones are the unit of care.
4. Psychological and spiritual pain are as significant as physical pain, and addressing all three requires the skills and approach of an interdisciplinary team.

5. Pain relief and symptom control are appropriate clinical goals; the goal of all intervention is to maximize the quality of remaining life through the provision of palliative therapies.

6. Care is provided regardless of ability to pay.

I will discuss these principles in turn. As to the first, it is important to distinguish three things that can be meant by the phrase "accepting death," a phrase that is very popular among hospice personnel. First is simply the having of true rather than false beliefs in this area, for example, the belief that death is a natural part of the life cycle in the sense of being inevitable, and, specifically for hospice patients, the belief that one has a terminal illness that is likely to cause death within a fairly short time. 'Accepting death,' in this sense, is *prima facie* desirable for the general reasons that true beliefs are better than false ones—the intrinsic reason that knowledge is *prima facie* better than error, and the extrinsic reason that one's plans are more likely to be satisfied if they are based on true beliefs rather than on false ones. But this superiority is only *prima facie* and hence can be overridden by other considerations, such as that some people would find some facts so painful to face that the benefits of believing what is true would not be worth it in these cases.

Could impending death be such a fact for some people? This question brings us to the second sense of "accepting death"—contemplating one's own impending death with serenity, rather than fear or resentment, and regarding "death as a friend," or at least reaching a "final stage [of] acceptance . . . not a resignation . . . but a real heartfelt feeling that what is happening is . . . not necessarily incorrect." Accepting death in this second sense obviously does not follow from accepting death in the first sense, nor does accepting death in the second sense have the first sense's assets of truth over falsity and rational belief over self-deception. Does it have anything to justify it?

Death and Serenity

In an interview shortly before his death, the terminally ill Joseph Cardinal Bernardin said, "I don't think I could be as tranquil [about my impending death] as I am if I didn't really believe [in an afterlife]." This raises some important questions. Although serenity in the face of impending death is reasonable for those who are confident they are going on to a better place, why should we expect such serenity from terminally ill people who believe their death will be "the unequivocal and permanent end of [their] existence"? Do such expectations constitute an attempt to export religiously based attitudes—attitudes that are reasonable when grounded in religious faith in the afterlife—into a context where the religious grounding that justifies these attitudes is lacking? These questions are especially important here because, although the National Hospice Organization's promotional material mentions that patients can "share their feelings" with "their own minister, priest, or rabbi [or] a chaplain, who may be part of the hospice team," the hospice movement is not officially religious and is intended to attract and care for nonreligious as well as religious people. But when people who do and those who do not believe in the afterlife talk about death, they are talking about entirely different things. For people who value their lives and do not believe in the afterlife, doesn't fearing death make perfect sense? We would be skeptical of people who claimed to value their marriages but faced the prospect of divorce serenely or who claimed to value their religious faith but were serene about the prospect of losing it. Why, then, should people who value their lives and do not believe in the afterlife be expected to face the loss of their lives with equanimity?

One popular sort of answer is that death is natural and that "renewal requires that death precede it so that the weary may be replaced by the vigorous. This is what is meant by the cycles of nature." Such a reason for serenity about one's own impending death requires great self-abnegation on the part of the terminally ill. This can hardly be attractive to people not inclined to such a sacrificial view of their own lives. As Thomas Nagel points out, the fact that death is natural is no proof against its being bad:

> Suppose that we were all inevitably going to die in *agony*—physical agony lasting six months. Would inevitability make *that* prospect any less unpleasant? And why should it be different for a deprivation? If the normal lifespan were a thou-

sand years, death at 80 would be a tragedy. As things are, it may just be a more widespread tragedy.

Questionable Ideology

Moreover, many hospice patients are facing death at an age far earlier than could be considered 'natural.' All these considerations point toward the following conclusion: the idea that people should face death with serenity, rather than, for example, following Dylan Thomas's famous advice to "Rage, rage against the dying of the light" illustrates my earlier claim that the National Hospice Organization's "philosophy of hospice" includes principles that rest on a highly questionable ideology that, while valuable for some terminally ill people, can reasonably be rejected by others. Hospice officials sometimes fail to recognize this, displaying instead the rigidity characteristic of people with fixed ideologies. For example, Ira Bates, former vice president of Programs/Services for the National Hospice Organization, disparages terminal patients who do not want hospice care as not being "ready for Hospice." On the other hand, Susan Buckley and Joan Richardson of the National Hospice Organization each answered "No" to my question, "Is hospice care what everyone wants or ought to want?"

The third sense of "accepting death" is that embodied in Principle 2 above, i.e., choosing to forgo all life-prolonging treatment or attempts at cure, as opposed to comfort care. It is important to recognize that 'accepting death' in this third sense follows neither from accepting death in the first sense nor even from accepting death in the second sense. So it needs its own separate treatment, to which I now turn in connection with my discussion of Principle 2 of the National Hospice Organization's "philosophy of hospice."

As it stands, Principle 2 is poorly formulated. Death is inevitable for everyone. Does this mean that the National Hospice Organization's "philosophy of hospice" rejects such life-prolonging measures as insulin or blood-pressure pills for people who are not terminally ill? Obviously not; this principle is intended to apply only to the sort of patient a hospice would admit in the first place—one who is terminally ill. . . . Even so, the principle is problematic. First, it does not indicate what counts as "postponing death" and why. Bringing food to the bedside of a bedridden patient? Feeding by hand a patient who can swallow but is too weak to lift a fork? Feeding intravenously or via a feeding tube? Elsewhere, the National Hospice Organization defines "prolongation of life" as "[u]sing artificial or other medical means to extend a patient's life beyond what would otherwise be the time of natural death," but it is still not entirely clear what this amounts to. Furthermore, the rationale for the principle is unclear. Hospice care can occur in the home (the most usual setting), or in a hospital-based unit, nursing home, or free-standing hospice facility. All these settings are generally well-equipped with air conditioning and central heating, electric lights, and windowshades. Clearly, hospice philosophy is not adverse to hastening or postponing the onset of indoor light, darkness, warmth, or coolness. Why does the National Hospice Organization regard death differently? Why does its "philosophy of hospice" include what might be called a "Goldilocks Principle" for terminal illness (death by assisted suicide is too soon, death after high-tech life-prolonging treatment is too late, "natural" death is just right), when hospices do not eschew intervention through technology or other forms of human ingenuity in other areas?

One possible rationale might be religious—God has determined when we are to die, and hence death should neither be hastened nor staved off by "artificial" means. The National Hospice Organization does not offer this sort of rationale. As I have mentioned, hospices are intended to attract and care for nonreligious as well as religious people. Moreover, such a rationale would be hard to sustain in light of hospice practice, as it would require an account of why God is willing to have us "artificially" extend the duration of light in a room but not the length of our lives.

High-Tech Care Versus Humane Care

Another possible rationale is that hospice caters to terminally ill people who want to die as soon as possible, but who have scruples, religious or otherwise, against suicide. But why do these people want to die as soon as possible? One answer might be that they have (or fear) intractable pain or a low

Hospice Care and Regulatory Red Tape

The federal government, through the Medicare program, pays for three-quarters of hospice care. . . .

But with government involvement [in hospice] has come unending regulatory red tape and episodes of purported abuse. As a result of regulations written into the Balanced Budget Act of 1997, patients must be within six months of death to be admitted to hospice. In addition, a patient or the patient's family must provide two letters from their doctors attesting to the terminal nature of their illness and the patient's understanding that active curative care must be forgone. The regulation is intended to prevent use of hospice by persons who should be in other programs. But does the regulation give hospice providers an incentive to hope for death?

In cases in which an individual survives past six months, the federal government fines the hospice $50,000 for perpetrating abuse of the program. Since 1995, according to an Office of the Inspector General report, only 15 percent of those admitted nationwide survive more than six months. But pockets of abuse do occur. A 1997 review of hospice facilities in four states found that 65.1 percent of patients participating weren't terminally ill, resulting in $83 million in inappropriate payments. . . .

The unintended result is that operators of nonprofit hospices fear they will be obliged to reimburse the costs in cases which are disputed. Therefore, some are less willing to take in patients [with AIDS and other terminal illnesses] who are not dying quickly enough.

Jennifer G. Hickey, *Insight on the News*, January 25, 1999.

"quality of life." These, however, are precisely the sorts of problems hospices claim to be able to alleviate. If hospices can make a terminally ill patient's life so high-quality and comfortable, why are they so adverse to prolonging it? An obvious reply is that some life-prolonging treatments are painful or otherwise unpleasant. But a nonideological organization would allow each patient to consider each possible life-prolonging medical treatment individually to decide for himself whether the possible discomfort is worth the prolonged life (and some such treatments, such as lifesaving antibiotics for pneumonia, may not be uncomfortable at all), instead of categorically refusing to provide treatment whose sole aim is life prolongation, as stated in Principle 2. This is another example of a National Hospice Organization principle that rests on a highly questionable ideology that many terminally ill patients can and do quite reasonably find unacceptable. Claims that "humane care [rather than] high-tech care . . . is what patients want and need" beg the question and obscure the issue by setting up a false dichotomy between humane care and high-tech care, overlooking the fact that for patients who want to prolong their lives and need high-tech care in order to do so, high-tech care *is* humane care.

Such patients are far from rare. Several recent studies have concluded that "many healthy people often say they would never want to die in an intensive care unit, but may change their minds when they are very sick . . . seriously ill . . . patients [are frequently] willing to grasp at any hope for a prolonged life.". . .

Many high-tech life-prolonging treatments, such as ventilators, can be used in home settings. Moreover, such claims as that hospice is "the most effective route to a dignified death" reveal a bigoted and superficial view of human dignity, as they imply that people who are disabled enough to need high-tech assistance in order to live have less human dignity than those who are able-bodied and healthy.

"The Paradox of the Selfless Invalid"

Of course, there is another possibility—that of a terminally ill patient who has scruples against suicide but who rejects high-tech life-prolonging or experimental curative treatment because he fears being a burden to his family or to society. But this further illustrates my point. Willingness to sacrifice what would otherwise be left of one's life in order to avoid burdening others is obviously a self-abnegating attitude many terminally ill people can reasonably reject. And the desire to forgo high-tech life-prolonging or experimental curative treatment in order to avoid being a burden specifically to one's loved ones raises an additional problem that I call "the paradox of the selfless invalid." That is, either the patient's loved ones want him to die quickly in order to preserve their inheritance or otherwise make their lives easier, or they do not. If they do not, the patient does them no favor by forgoing life-prolonging or experimental curative treatment for their sake. If they do, then why is the patient sacrificing what would otherwise be left of his life (or sacrificing his long-shot chance at a cure) for people who love him so little that they value his life less than their money or freedom from encumbrance? Wouldn't a truly loving family find such a sacrifice appalling? Of course, families can have mixed feelings, which include both the desire to have the patient stay alive and the self-interested desire to get it all over with and to keep expenses down. But the basic point remains. Decent and loving families, as part of their decency and lovingness, will recognize the latter desire as ignoble and, on balance, will not want patients to pander to it.

Favoring Families over Patients

This brings us naturally to a discussion of the third principle of the National Hospice Organization's "philosophy of hospice," the principle that patients, their families, and loved ones (rather than just the patients themselves) are the unit of care. Like the preceding two principles, this is a cornerstone of the hospice approach, and also like the preceding two principles, it is open to various interpretations. First, the most innocuous: Since "home is the usual care setting for hospice patients," hospice provides support for family caregivers. While this may seem unexceptionable, even here problems can arise, as the following case illustrates.

> When Patient X was diagnosed with terminal cancer in 1988, he chose hospice care, not because he was interested in receiving counseling to help him "accept death" or in discussing his personal feelings with strangers, but because he wanted to die at home and with as little pain as possible. He and his wife were told that hospice personnel normally could come to their home between 8 A.M. and 4:30 P.M. on weekdays, but were always available for house calls in an emergency. He was also given a prescription for oral morphine and told that should be adequate for pain control. The following week, when the patient suffered agonizing pain in the middle of the night (which turned out to be the last night of his life), the hospice failed to send anyone in response to his wife's numerous distress telephone calls, telling her later that she had not seemed upset enough for it to be an emergency. As she wrote in a letter to the hospice after her husband's death, "During my husband's illness, a great deal of attention

was focused on me . . . by Hospice . . . Everyone was sympathetic, and seemed quite anxious to do things for me . . . The trouble with all this sympathy is that, given your limited funds (and I must assume your funds are limited, everybody's are), it was directed toward the wrong person. I was perfectly healthy. My husband, on the other hand, was terribly sick. And I would gladly have forgone every sympathetic word, every hypothetical shoulder to cry on, every kind of 'support,' if only some nurse or doctor in your organization had just come out in the middle of the night when my husband was dying and given him something for his agony."

This case illustrates the point that despite the popular contemporary tendency to regard the suffering of the terminally ill and the suffering of their loved ones as on a par, they rarely are. The terminally ill patient is generally far worse off than his healthy (or at least healthier) family. A policy that abdicates medicine's traditional responsibility of putting the patient first, and instead diverts resources of time and attention from patient to family before the patient's genuine medical needs are met, risks shortchanging the dying at their time of greatest need. In recognition of these points, Principle 3 might be called "The Mrs. Ilych Principle," after the cancer patient's widow in Tolstoy's *The Death of Ivan Ilych*, who says, "For the last three days he screamed incessantly. It was unendurable. I cannot understand how I bore it; you could hear him three rooms off. Oh, what I have suffered!" Tolstoy evidently took this to indicate monumental callousness and self-centeredness. How would the hospice movement take it?

Principle 3 can be further problematic when interpreted another way. After all, although there is a sense in which "patients, their families and loved ones" are a unit, there is also a sense in which they are not. They are separate individuals with separate and possibly conflicting interests. Making patients, their families, and loved ones, rather than the patients themselves the unit of care risks glossing over these conflicts of interest or sacrificing the interests of the patients to the interests of their families. . . .

The thrust of this viewpoint has been to examine the principles of the National Hospice Organization's "philosophy of hospice" and to argue that several depend on a highly questionable ideology that many terminally ill people can and apparently do quite reasonably find unacceptable. Thus, when its principles are fully scrutinized and understood, hospice care will be seen, not as "the most effective route to a dignified death," but as just one option for the terminally ill, whose other options should include experimental attempts at a cure, high-tech life-prolongation, and perhaps even assisted suicide.

| *"Physicians [whose] patients [request assisted suicide] shouldn't be forced by legislative prohibition into covert actions."* |

Physician-Assisted Suicide Should Be Legalized

Peter Rogatz

In the following viewpoint, Peter Rogatz contends that physician-assisted suicide, illegal in every state except Oregon, should be legalized because every patient has the right to control his or her body and each physician has a duty to relieve suffering. Legalizing physician-assisted suicide will not lead to the deaths of vulnerable patients, such as the poor and elderly, if patients have to meet appropriate criteria before receiving assistance. According to Rogatz, simply managing pain and depression is not sufficient when an illness reduces a patient to a state of desperation. The author is a founding board member of Compassion in Dying of New York, an organization that supports humane aid in dying for the terminally ill.

As you read, consider the following questions:
1. In the author's opinion, what factors are recognized as more important than pain by patients who seek physician-assisted suicide?
2. What criteria does Rogatz assert patients should have to meet before receiving suicide assistance?
3. According to Rogatz, what things did not happen in the aftermath of the passage of Oregon's physician-assisted suicide law?

P hysician-assisted suicide is among the most hotly debated bioethical issues for our time. Every reasonable person prefers that no patient ever contemplate suicide—with or without assistance—and recent improvements in pain management have begun to reduce the number of patients seeking such assistance. However, there are some patients who experience terrible suffering that cannot be relieved by any of the therapeutic or palliative techniques that medicine and nursing have to offer and some of those patients desperately seek deliverance.

Patient Autonomy and Relief from Suffering

This is not about physicians being killers. It's about patients whose suffering we cannot relieve and about not turning away from them when they ask for help. Will there be physicians who feel they can't do this? Of course, and they shouldn't be obliged to. But if other physicians consider it merciful to help such patients by merely writing a prescription, it is unreasonable to place them in jeopardy of criminal prosecution, loss of license, or other penalty for doing so.

Many arguments are put forward for maintaining the prohibition against physician-assisted suicide, but I believe they are outweighed by two fundamental principles that support ending the prohibition: patient autonomy—the right to control one's own body—and the physician's duty to relieve suffering.

Society recognizes the competent patient's right to autonomy—to decide what will or won't be done to his or her body. There is almost universal agreement that a competent adult has the right to self-determination, including the right to have life-sustaining treatment withheld or withdrawn. Suicide, once illegal throughout the United States, is no longer illegal in any part of the country. Yet assisting a person to take her or his own life is prohibited in every state but Oregon. If patients seek such help, it is cruel to leave them to fend for themselves, weighing options that are both traumatic and uncertain, when humane assistance could be made available.

The physician's obligations are many but, when cure is impossible and palliation has failed to achieve its objectives, there is always a residual obligation to relieve suffering. Ultimately, if the physician has exhausted all reasonable palliative measures, it is the patient—and only the patient—who can judge whether death is harmful or a good to be sought. Marcia Angell, former executive editor of the *New England Journal of Medicine*, has put it this way:

> The highest ethical imperative of doctors should be to provide care in whatever way best serves patients' interests, in accord with each patient's wishes, not with a theoretical commitment to preserve life no matter what the cost in suffering. . . . The greatest harm we can do is to consign a desperate patient to unbearable suffering—or force the patient to seek out a stranger like Dr. Kevorkian.

A Merciful End

Let's examine the key arguments made against physician-assisted suicide. First, much weight is placed on the Hippocratic injunction to do no harm. It has been asserted that sanctioning physician-assisted suicide "would give doctors a license to kill," and physicians who accede to such requests have been branded by some as murderers. This is both illogical and inflammatory. Withdrawal of life-sustaining treatment—for example, disconnecting a ventilator at a patient's request—is accepted by society, yet this requires a more definitive act by a physician than prescribing a medication that a patient has requested and is free to take or not, as he or she sees fit. Why should the latter be perceived as doing harm when the former is not? Rather than characterizing this as "killing," we should see it as bringing the dying process to a merciful end. The physician who complies with a plea for final release from a patient facing death under unbearable conditions is doing good, not harm, and her or his actions are entirely consonant with the Hippocratic tradition.

Second, it is argued that requests for assisted suicide come largely from patients who haven't received adequate pain control or who are clinically depressed and haven't been properly diagnosed or treated. There is no question that proper management of such conditions would significantly reduce the number of patients who consider suicide; any sanctioning of assistance should be contingent upon prior management of pain and depression.

However, treatable pain is not the only reason, or even the most common reason, why patients seek to end their lives.

Severe body wasting, intractable vomiting, urinary and bowel incontinence, immobility, and total dependence are recognized as more important than pain in the desire for hastened death. There is a growing awareness that loss of dignity and of those attributes that we associate particularly with being human are the factors that most commonly reduce patients to a state of unrelieved misery and desperation.

Enhancing Trust

Third, it is argued that permitting physician-assisted suicide would undermine the sense of trust that patients have in their doctors. This is curious reasoning; patients are not lying in bed wondering if their physicians are going to kill them—and permitting assisted suicide shouldn't create such fears, since the act of administering a fatal dose would be solely within the control of the patient. Rather than undermining a patient's trust, I would expect the legalization of physician-assisted suicide to enhance that trust. I have spoken with a great many people who feel that they would like to be able to trust their physicians to provide such help in the event of unrelieved suffering—and making that possible would give such patients a greater sense of security. Furthermore, some patients have taken their own lives at a relatively early stage of terminal illness precisely because they feared that progressively increasing disability, without anyone to assist them, would rob them of this option at a later time when they were truly desperate. A patient contemplating suicide would be much less likely to take such a step if he or she were confident of receiving assistance in the future if so desired.

Fourth, it is argued that patients don't need assistance to commit suicide; they can manage it all by themselves. This seems both callous and unrealistic. Are patients to shoot themselves, jump from a window, starve themselves to death, or rig a pipe to the car exhaust? All of these methods have been used by patients in the final stages of desperation, but it is a hideous experience for both patient and survivors. Even patients who can't contemplate such traumatic acts and instead manage to hoard a supply of lethal drugs may be too weak to complete the process without help and therefore face a high risk of failure, with dreadful consequences for themselves and their families.

Fifth, it is argued that requests for assisted suicide are not frequent enough to warrant changing the law. Interestingly, some physicians say they have rarely, if ever, received such requests, while others say they have often received requests. This is a curious discrepancy, but I think it can be explained: the patient who seeks help with suicide will cautiously test a physician's receptivity to the idea and simply won't approach a physician who is unreceptive. Thus, there are two subsets of physicians in this situation: those who are open to the idea of assisted suicide and those who aren't. Patients are likely to seek help from the former but not from the latter.

A study carried out a few years ago by the University of Washington School of Medicine queried 828 physicians (a 25 percent sample of primary care physicians and all physicians in selected medical subspecialties) with a response rate of 57 percent. Of these respondents, 12 percent reported receiving one or more explicit requests for assisted suicide, and one-fourth of the patients requesting such assistance received prescriptions.

A survey of physicians in San Francisco treating AIDS patients brought responses from half, and 53 percent of those respondents reported helping patients take their own lives by prescribing lethal doses of narcotics. Clearly, requests for assisted suicide can't be dismissed as rare occurrences.

Sixth, it is argued that sanctioning assisted suicide would fail to address the needs of patients who are incompetent. This is obviously true, since proposals for legalization specify that assistance be given only to a patient who is competent and who requests it. However, in essence, this argument says that, because we can't establish a procedure that will deal with every patient, we won't make assisted suicide available to any patient. What logic! Imagine the outcry if that logic were applied to a procedure such as organ transplantation, which has benefited so many people in this country.

Grappling with the "Slippery Slope"
Seventh, it is argued that once we open the door to physician-assisted suicide we will find ourselves on a slippery slope leading to coercion and involuntary euthanasia of vulnerable pa-

tients. Why so? We have learned to grapple with many slippery slopes in medicine—such as Do Not Resuscitate (DNR) orders and the withdrawal of life support. We don't deal with those slippery slopes by prohibition but, rather, by adopting reasonable ground rules and setting appropriate limits.

The slippery slope argument discounts the real harm of failing to respond to the pleas of real people and considers only the potential harm that might be done to others at some future time and place. As in the case of other slippery slopes, theoretical future harm can be mitigated by establishing appropriate criteria that would have to be met before a patient could receive assistance. Such criteria have been outlined frequently. Stated briefly, they include:

1. The patient must have an incurable condition causing severe, unrelenting suffering.

2. The patient must understand his or her condition and prognosis, which must be verified by an independent second opinion.

3. All reasonable palliative measures must have been presented to and considered by the patient.

4. The patient must clearly and repeatedly request assistance in dying.

5. A psychiatric consultation must be held to establish if the patient is suffering from a treatable depression.

6. The prescribing physician, absent a close preexisting relationship (which would be ideal), must get to know the patient well enough to understand the reasons for her or his request.

7. No physician should be expected to violate his or her own basic values. A physician who is unwilling to assist the patient should facilitate transfer to another physician who would be prepared to do so.

8. All of the foregoing must be clearly documented.

Application of the above criteria would substantially reduce the risk of abuse but couldn't guarantee that abuse would never occur. We must recognize, however, that abuses occur today—in part because we tolerate covert action that is subject to no safeguards at all. A more open process would, in the words of philosopher and ethicist Margaret Battin, "prod us to develop much stronger protections for the kinds of choices about death we already make in what are often quite casual, cavalier ways."

It seems improbable that assisted suicide would pose a special danger to the elderly, infirm, and disabled. To paraphrase John Maynard Keynes, in the long run we are all elderly, infirm, or disabled and, since society well knows this, serious attention would surely be given to adequate protections against abuse. It isn't my intention to dispose glibly of the fear that society would view vulnerable patients as a liability and would manipulate them to end their lives prematurely. Of course, this concern must be respected, but the risk can be minimized by applying the criteria listed above. Furthermore, this argument assumes that termination of life is invariably an evil against which we must protect vulnerable patients who are poor or otherwise lacking in societal support. But, by definition, we are speaking of patients who desperately wish final release from unrelieved suffering, and poor and vulnerable patients are least able to secure aid in dying if they want it. The well-to-do patient may, with some effort and some good luck, find a physician who is willing to provide covert help; the poor and disenfranchised rarely have access to such assistance in today's world.

Avoiding Abuses

Eighth, it is argued that the Netherlands experience proves that societal tolerance of physician-assisted suicide leads to serious abuse. Aside from the fact that the data are subject to varying interpretation depending upon which analysis one believes, the situation in the Netherlands holds few lessons for us, because for many years that country followed the ambiguous practice of technically prohibiting but tacitly permitting assisted suicide and euthanasia.

The climate in the United States is different; our regulatory mechanisms would be different—much stricter, of course—and we should expect different outcomes. The experience of Oregon—the only one of our fifty states to permit physician-assisted suicide—is instructive. During the first three years that Oregon's law has been in effect, seventy terminally ill patients took advantage of the opportunity to self-administer medication to end protracted dying. Despite dire warnings, there was no precipitous rush by Oregonians to embrace assisted suicide. The poor and the uninsured weren't victimized; almost all of these seventy patients had health insurance, most were on hospice care, and most were people with at least some college education. There were no untoward complications. The Oregon experience is far more relevant for the United States than the Dutch experience, and it vindicates those who, despite extremely vocal opposition, advocated for the legislation.

Wilkenson. © 1995 by *Philadelphia Daily News*. Reprinted by permission of the cartoonist and Writers Syndicate.

Ninth, it has been argued that a society that doesn't assure all its citizens the right to basic health care and protect them against catastrophic health costs has no business considering physician-assisted suicide. I find this an astonishing argument. It says to every patient who seeks ultimate relief from severe suffering that his or her case won't be considered until all of us are assured basic health care and financial protection. These are certainly proper goals for any decent society, but they won't be attained in the United States until it becomes a more generous and responsible nation—and that day seems to be far off. Patients seeking deliverance from unrelieved suffering shouldn't be held hostage pending hoped-for future developments that are not even visible on the distant horizon.

Rejecting the Status Quo

Finally, it is argued that the status quo is acceptable—that a patient who is determined to end his or her life can find a sympathetic physician who will provide the necessary prescription and that physicians are virtually never prosecuted for such acts. There are at least four reasons to reject the status quo. First, it forces patients and physicians to undertake a clandestine conspiracy to violate the law, thus compromising the integrity of patient, physician, and family. Second, such secret compacts, by their very nature, are subject to faulty implementation with a high risk of failure and consequent tragedy for both patient and family. Third, the assumption that a determined patient can find a sympathetic physician applies, at best, to middle- and upper-income persons who have ongoing relationships with their physicians; the poor, as I've already noted, rarely have such an opportunity. Fourth, covert action places a physician in danger of criminal prosecution or loss of license and, although such penalties are assumed to be unlikely, that risk certainly inhibits some physicians from doing what they believe is proper to help their patients.

I believe that removing the prohibition against physician assistance, rather than opening the flood gates to ill-advised suicides, is likely to reduce the incentive for suicide: patients who fear great suffering in the final stages of illness would have the assurance that help would be available if needed and they would be more inclined to test their own abilities to withstand the trials that lie ahead.

Life is the most precious gift of all, and no sane person wants to part with it, but there are some circumstances where life has lost its value. A competent person who has thoughtfully considered his or her own situation and finds that unrelieved suffering outweighs the value of continued life shouldn't have to starve to death or find other drastic and violent solutions when more merciful means exist. Those physicians who wish to fulfill what they perceive to be their humane responsibilities to their patients shouldn't be forced by legislative prohibition into covert actions.

There is no risk-free solution to these very sensitive problems. However, I believe that reasonable protections can be put in place that will minimize the risk of abuse and that the humanitarian benefits of legalizing physician-assisted suicide outweigh that risk. All physicians are bound by the injunction to do no harm, but we must recognize that harm may result not only from the commission of a wrongful act but also from the omission of an act of mercy. While not every physician will feel comfortable offering help in these tragic situations, many believe it is right to do so and our society should not criminalize such humanitarian acts.

"Beneath the propaganda of compassion . . . assisted suicide is purely and simply about making people dead."

Physician-Assisted Suicide Should Not Be Legalized

Wesley J. Smith

In 1997, Oregon became the first and only U.S. state to legalize physician-assisted suicide. In the following viewpoint, Wesley J. Smith argues that physicians should not be permitted to cause the deaths of patients by using lethal injections or any other means. Advocates of assisted suicide have attempted to legitimize their cause by promoting it as mainstream medical reform and using the authority of physicians. Once legitimized, however, the author warns that advocates will expand the list of those considered eligible for assisted suicide to include the elderly, depressed, or disabled. Smith is an attorney for the International Anti-Euthanasia Task Force and the author of *Culture of Death: The Assault on Medical Ethics in America*.

As you read, consider the following questions:

1. How is the death of the Heaven's Gate cultists identical to legalized physician-assisted suicide, in the author's opinion?
2. What proof does Smith offer in defense of his contention that assisted-suicide advocates wish to expand killing beyond the terminally ill?
3. According to the author, how does the assisted-suicide movement impede the efforts of doctors to control their patients' pain?

Assisted-suicide patriarch Derek Humphry was impressed with the suicide machines unveiled in Seattle on November 13, 1999 at the international "Self-Deliverance New Technology Conference." He loved the demonstration on the use of helium and a garbage bag to commit suicide, a method that Humphry, author of *How to Commit Suicide* and co-founder of the Hemlock Society, extols in his newest how-to-end-it-all video. But he was most delighted with a new suicide contraption called "the debreather," a device developed under the aegis of Canadian assisted-suicide zealot John Hofsess, that is worn like a gas mask but which sucks away life by removing oxygen from the air of the person wearing it. Humphry happily reported that the debreather has killed six people.

Celebrating Death Devices

Other assisted-suicide movement notables were equally enthusiastic about the conference and the devices on display. Faye Girsh, the executive director of the Hemlock Society USA, called the meeting a "wonderful forum," and proclaimed herself deeply impressed by the "tremendous ingenuity" displayed by the inventors. The Dutch doctor Peter Admiraal, who admits to having killed more than 100 of his patients, also expressed his satisfaction with the displays. Australian doctor Dr. Philip Nitschke—the Down-Under [Jack] Kevorkian [a U.S. assisted-suicide advocate]—who in 1999 was in the midst of a North American assisted-suicide-promotion speaking tour, thrilled the conventioneers with a description of his pet project: the still uncompleted creation of a non-narcotic death pill that he calls the "Holy Grail." Once he gets the kinks worked out, Nitschke intends to sell the lethal pill internationally over the Internet.

The debreather is not the first suicide device publicized and marketed by the assisted-suicide movement. For example, a few years ago the "Exit Bag" made its debut. The Exit Bag, described by its promoters as a "hand-made customized plastic bag for use in self-deliverance [i.e., suicide]," is sold by mail—no questions asked. (I bought one for $44, which included illustrated suicide instructions and postage.) The Exit Bag's promotional material enthusiastically extols the product's many alleged virtues:

The Exit Bag is made of clear strong industrial plastic. It has an adjustable collar . . . for a snug but comfortable fit. It is extra large (22" × 36") to reduce heat build-up. It comes with flannelette lining inside the collar so that the plastic won't irritate sensitive skin. AND it comes with an optional terry-cloth neckband to create a "turtleneck" for added comfort and snugness of fit. (This is particularly useful for terminally ill people who have lost a lot of weight and neck bulk.) Discreetly shipped.

Making People Dead

For years, euthanasia enthusiasts have desperately attempted to reposition the movement away from its well-deserved place among the nut fringe by creating the fiction that it is merely promoting mainstream "medical" reform. At best, that is veneer. Beneath the propaganda of compassion and the obfuscating buzzwords for killing such as "aid in dying," assisted suicide is purely and simply about making people dead. Indeed, just like any suicide cult, death—not quality health care—is the movement's all-encompassing obsession. The convention and the Exit Bag are pertinent reminders of this overriding truth.

Remember the mass suicide of the Heaven's Gate cult in 1997? It is worth remembering that the lives of the UFO-obsessed cultists all ended identically to those who died in Oregon by legalized physician-assisted suicide. The method of dying in Heaven's Gate and Oregon was identical, i.e., swallowing a mass overdose of barbiturates. The cause of death—a massive drug overdose—is also the same. The reason for "choosing" assisted suicide was similar too: a belief that life no longer had any quality, a feeling of terminal ennui among cultists that is close to the fear of becoming a burden exhibited by those with terminal illness in Oregon.

With the methods, causes, and fundamental reasoning behind the Heaven's Gate deaths virtually identical with those occurring in Oregon, the only clear distinction that can be drawn between the two circumstances is the participation by doctors in the latter category and the lack of medical involvement in the former. Thus, either the cultists were illegally practicing medicine when they obtained the drugs for use in overdosing and committing their assisted suicides, or

Oregon doctors who knowingly prescribe lethal doses of drugs, intended to kill their patients, aren't engaged in a bona fide medical act at all.

False Logic

Which is it? Let's explore the issue further. An Oregon doctor who prescribes an intentionally lethal overdose at the request of a patient who wants to die because of a business failure would be guilty of a felony. If the doctor prescribes a lethal overdose for someone who wants to die because their children have been killed in an auto accident, he would be guilty of a felony. Indeed, if a lethal prescription were given because the patient had a difficult or chronic but non-terminal illness, the doctor would be just as guilty as in the first two cases. But if the same doctor issued the same prescription for the same person who wanted to die for the same reasons but who had also been, coincidentally, diagnosed with terminal cancer, suddenly the act of prescribing a lethal overdose is "practicing medicine." The logic fails. Either all of these hypothetical prescriptions are medical acts or none are.

Assisted-suicide advocates would at this point undoubtedly claim that it is precisely the presence of a terminal illness that transforms the normally criminal and wrongful act of assisted suicide into a beneficent medical procedure. But that is disingenuous. Proponents of assisted suicide have no intention of strictly limiting eligibility for their services to people with terminal conditions. However, they do take polls and conduct focus groups from which they have concluded that the public is very uncomfortable with legalizing assisted suicide when those who may be killed legally include people who are chronically ill, elderly, depressed, or disabled. Thus, advocates limit their public advocacy to terminal illness as a political tactic, not a moral conviction.

Expanding the "Mission"

Proof of this deep strategy abounds for anyone interested in looking for it. In December 1997, just after the Oregon death law went into effect, the misnamed Compassion in Dying (CID) [an assisted-suicide advocacy group], in Washington, released a fund-raising letter claiming that donations

Depression, Losing Control, and Assisted Suicide

Like other suicidal individuals, patients who desire an early death during a serious or terminal illness are usually suffering from a treatable depressive condition. Although pain and other factors such as lack of family support contribute to the wish for death, recent research has confirmed that none is as significant as the presence of depression, which researchers have found to be the only predictor of the desire for death.

Both patients who attempt suicide and those who request assisted suicide often test the affection and care of others, confiding feelings like "I don't want to be a burden to my family" or "My family would be better off without me." Such statements are classic indicators of suicidal depression. . . .

Unfortunately, depression itself is commonly underdiagnosed and often inadequately treated. Although most people who kill themselves are under medical care at the time of death, their physicians often fail to recognize the symptoms of depressive illness or, even if they do, fail to give adequate treatment.

The fact that a patient finds relief in the prospect of death is not a sign that the decision is appropriate. Patients who are depressed and suicidal may appear calm and less depressed after deciding to end their lives, whether by themselves or with the help of a doctor. It is coping with the uncertainties of life that agitate and depress them. . . .

Patients are not alone in their inability to tolerate situations they cannot control. Lewis Thomas has written insightfully about the sense of failure and helplessness that doctors may experience in the face of death; such feelings may explain why doctors have such difficulty discussing terminal illness with patients.

By deciding when patients die, by making death a medical decision, the physician preserves the illusion of mastery over the disease and the accompanying feelings of helplessness. The physician, not the illness, is responsible for the death. Assisting suicide and euthanasia become ways of dealing with the frustration of not being able to cure the disease.

Herbert Hendin, *Seduced by Death: Doctors, Patients, and Assisted Suicide*, 1998.

were needed more urgently than ever. Having been a key player in legalizing assisted suicide in Oregon, CID leaders should have been satisfied that their work was essentially done. They weren't. With Oregon safely under their belts, the suicide advocates were now ready to move their death agenda to the next level. More funds were needed, the leaders wrote because, "We have expanded our mission to include not only terminally ill individuals, but also persons with incurable illnesses which will eventually lead to a terminal diagnosis." Similarly, on July 27, 1998, the Hemlock Society, perhaps the nation's largest assisted-suicide advocacy group, issued a press release calling for the legalization of assisted suicide for people with "incurable conditions."

The use of the terms "incurable" and "hopeless illness," by these groups and other advocates, to describe those who should have access to assisted-suicide is intentional. This is language-parsing, designed to give the false impression that the subject has a terminal illness when it really isn't. After all, many incurable conditions do not lead to death. Arthritis is incurable. Paraplegia may not be capable of amelioration. Herpes too is incurable, as is asymptomatic HIV infection, multiple sclerosis, diabetes, emphysema, asthma, and myriad other diseases. Depression might be incurable. Words have meaning but they are used more often to obfuscate in assisted-suicide advocacy than to edify.

That is not to say that movement activists are never candid. Once in a great while they forget themselves and allow the true agenda to come into rare focus. One such occasion came about in October 1998, when the World Federation of Right to Die Societies—an international umbrella organization consisting of the world's foremost euthanasia advocacy groups—issued its "Zurich Declaration" after its bi-annual convention. The Declaration urged that people "suffering severe and enduring distress [should be eligible] to receive medical help to die." (My emphasis.) By definition, anybody with a significant suicidal desire has enduring distress! Finally, the goal of the assisted-suicide movement is revealed in all its bleak nihilism: death on demand for anyone with more than a transitory desire to die.

Pushed into this corner, advocates might claim that a desire "to suicide" (many advocates, including some mental health professionals, have taken to using the term as a verb) is sometimes "rational," and when it is, the proper response is medical facilitation. The comparison is to the medical response to severe pain in which a doctor may prescribe morphine. Pain control is a legitimate medical act but the same prescription for a patient who wants the drugs merely to get high would not be. Thus, according to this argument, assisted suicide is akin to pain control with intentional life termination legitimately medical in some cases but not in others.

Using the Authority of "Medicine"

That brings us back full-circle to the Self-Deliverance Technology Convention and the Exit Bag. Ask yourselves these questions: Is the "debreather" a medical device that should be licensed by the government? Is helium a palliative agent? Should health insurance or Medicare cover the Exit Bag's cost? It seems to me that any reasonable person would say no. Now, ask yourself this: are these approaches to ending life different in any meaningful or substantive way from swallowing prescribed poison or being injected with a lethal drug? I submit that they are not. They are merely differing methods toward the same end—killing. A doctor's participation in causing death by poison is no more a medical treatment than would be Derek Humphry's placing the debreather over a suicidal person's face.

So what is the point of doctors' involvement in assisted suicide? Lending an appearance of respectability to an unconscionable act. Advocates know that their ad hoc approach to killing will never catch on. However, they also know that the public, lawmakers, and judges tend to defer in matters involving health care public policy to the medical profession. Thus, if they can invoke the physician's authority in medicalizing killing and using the authority of "medicine" to cause death, assisted-suicide advocates hope to overcome society's resistance to their agenda. It is akin to painting a dung beetle yellow and black and calling it a monarch butterfly: changing the appearance does not alter the reality.

Impeding Improved Pain Control

The inroads made by the assisted-suicide movement is testimony less to its legitimacy than to the deep dissatisfaction many people have with the current state of American medicine. The sad fact is that doctors generally do a poor job of controlling their patients' pain and providing dying people with quality end-of-life care. Much work must be done to alleviate these deficiencies. Unfortunately, the assisted-suicide movement impedes these efforts by distracting the media from focusing on all that medicine can and should do to alleviate suffering and misdirecting it instead toward the more news-exploitable issue of killing. This is how Jack Kevorkian became one of the most famous non-doctors in the world. At the same time, most people who would name Kevorkian easily in a trivia contest don't even know who Dame Cecily Saunders is. Yet Dr. Saunders created the modern hospice movement, which through its intense focus on controlling the symptoms of dying people, is directly responsible for helping millions worldwide meet their natural ends peacefully, comfortably, and with the kind of dignity that a forced exit never provides.

Turning the Tide

The good news is that the tide is slowly turning against assisted suicide and moving in the direction of improving the delivery of quality medical care. For example, the House of Representatives passed the Pain Relief Promotion Act (PRPA) by a bipartisan 271–156 vote, a bill that would improve the delivery of pain control while deterring assisted suicide. The PRPA is supported by much of organized medicine, including the American Medical Association and the National Hospice Organization. If passed by the Senate and signed by President Clinton, the act will both deter assisted suicide and improve the delivery of pain control by explicitly identifying palliation as a legitimate medical service under the Controlled Substances Act, thereby removing the fear of DEA actions against doctors who aggressively treat pain. Moreover, several states have recently outlawed assisted suicide or added civil penalties to anyone assisting a suicide, while at the same time making it clear that aggressive palliation that leads to the unintended side effect of death is not a crime. These laws have led directly to a dramatic increase in the delivery of quality pain control wherever they have been passed, thereby disproving the canard of assisted-suicide advocates that legalization of killing is necessary to improve medical caring.

The Self-Deliverance New Technology Conference cast a much-needed light on the twisted mindset that drives the assisted-suicide movement. Killing devices are not akin to kidney dialysis machines and poison is not medicine. The Heaven's Gate cultists were not practicing medicine when they helped each other commit assisted suicide and neither are doctors who participate in intentionally killing their patients. The time has come to turn away from the quackery of assisted suicide, increase the use of hospice, and support actions that improve the delivery of legitimate, quality medical care for all suffering people.

*"[Without advance directives] you may find
your control over the circumstances of your
death slipping away from you."*

Advance Directives Enable Dying Patients to Control Treatment

David Kessler

Advance directives are written instructions that a person can prepare for doctors and family members describing what treatments to administer or withhold in the event of a terminal illness, coma, or other incapacitating health crisis. The living will and durable power of attorney for health care are two types of advance directives. David Kessler asserts in the following viewpoint that advance directives enable people to make their end-of-life care wishes clearly known and can prevent unwanted or "heroic" measures to prolong life. As a result, patients have more control over their deaths. Kessler is the author of *The Rights of the Dying: A Companion for Life's Final Moments.*

As you read, consider the following questions:

1. As reported by the author, how does Dr. Katz's experience with a dying patient make a strong case for the importance of advance directives?
2. What is the proxy's role in safeguarding a person's end-of-life care wishes, according to Katz?
3. In the author's opinion, why should patients choose a doctor who shares their values and beliefs?

E veryone has read in the newspapers of families going to court to force the doctors to remove the respirator from their loved one who has been lying in a coma for years. These legal battles can rage for months, ripping families apart, possibly forcing patients to remain "alive" against their wishes. The key issue is always the patient's wishes. Most people never make their wishes known. Mrs. Smith may think that her husband, who is now in a coma, wanted to go quickly and quietly, while her son believes that his father wanted to die fighting. When we can't ask Mr. Smith what he wants, we have to turn to lawyers and judges who have never met Mr. Smith and can't possibly know what he wants done.

Respecting Wishes

Most people simply don't want to talk about death and dying. Talking about it means facing the fact that we or someone we love will die someday, perhaps soon. Sometimes we are even afraid that talking about it may make it happen. Many remain silent until they can no longer speak. Then someone else must make a choice and decide whether to keep the respirator and the other machines on or to switch them off. The choice usually falls to women, for they tend to outlive their husbands. Many women struggle to hold firm to their opinions in the face of strong-willed male physicians who have different ideas. Your wishes may not be respected if you make them known only to your spouse. . . .

Emergency room physician Dr. Mark Katz deals with patients who haven't had time to express their wishes. He told me about a patient he treated one hectic day. Seriously ill, dazed, and unable to communicate, the man tried to push Mark's hand away as he struggled to insert a breathing tube into the patient's throat. He couldn't tell if the patient was trying to indicate that he didn't want any more care or if he was trying to swat away the uncomfortable instrument being stuck into his mouth because he didn't realize what was happening. Was it simply an unconscious reflex? "There was no way to know," Dr. Katz said sadly. "At the tail end of his life the man was unable to make his wishes known, and unable to choose the how, when, and where of his death."

We *can* make our wishes known, but so many of us are reluctant to do so simply because we don't want to address the issue. Others are afraid if they make their wishes known they will receive inferior care, or no care at all. This is very common among people traditionally underserved by the medical system. But if today we don't face the fact that we will die someday, we may find ourselves powerless to change what is happening to us tomorrow.

Advanced Directives

If you find it difficult to talk about your wishes, you can express them on paper via documents known as an Advanced Directives [also known as a "living will"] or Durable Power of Attorney for Health Care. These documents speak for you when you cannot. They allow you to specify the level of treatment you wish to receive, anything from full heroic measures to nothing but painkillers to keep you comfortable as you pass on. You can also designate a proxy, a person who will make decisions for you when you cannot. This sample Advanced Directives put out by the California Medical Association offers three options from which you can choose:

> I do not want efforts made to prolong my life and I do not want life-sustaining treatment to be provided or continued: (1) If I am in an irreversible coma or persistent vegetative state: or (2) If I am terminally ill and the application of life-sustaining procedures would serve only to artificially delay the moment of my death: or (3) Under any other circumstances where the burdens of the treatment outweigh the expected benefits. I want my agent to consider the relief of suffering and the quality as well as the extent of the possible extension of my life in making decisions concerning life-sustaining treatment.

or

> I want efforts made to prolong my life and I want life-sustaining treatment to be provided unless I am in a coma or persistent vegetative state which my doctor reasonably believes to be irreversible. Once my doctor has concluded that I will remain unconscious for the rest of my life, I do not want life-sustaining treatment to be provided or continued.

> I want efforts made to prolong my life and I want life-sustaining treatment to be provided even if I am in an irreversible coma or persistent vegetative state. . . .

Selecting a Representative

It's important to select a strong representative to safeguard your wishes, someone who will stand up for you, under pressure, even if they disagree with your decision. Your first instinct may be to assign that responsibility to the person closest to you, but that person is not always strong or decisive enough to carry out your requests. It's also vital that you discuss your wishes with this person *before* designating him or her as your proxy. Express your feelings clearly. Let her know that you consider her help to be an act of love. Emphasize that she is *giving* you something, not taking anything away. Emphasize that the *disease* will kill you, not the directives, not the decision she may be called upon to make.

It is natural to feel guilty about turning off respirators or other medical equipment. Many people say, "I want them to

Active Treatments or "Comfort Only" Care?

Percentage of patients* (n=74) who would not want active treatments for any additional illness (for example, pneumonia) if they had disabilities. The diagonal gives the percentage of participants preferring "comfort only" care should they have one of seven disabilities and the other results refer to a combination of two of them.

Disability	Unable to speak	In a wheelchair	Bed bound	Fed by percutaneous endoscopic gastrostomy	Advanced dementia	Blind	Doubly incontinent
Unable to speak	52						
In a wheelchair	64	24					
Bed bound	78	NA	58				
Fed by percutaneous endoscopic gastrostomy	77	74	81	57			
Advanced dementia	90	83	92	90	78		
Blind	82	78	82	79	88	44	
Doubly incontinent	82	76	81	79	89	82	53

NA = not applicable.

*This table shows the results of a questionnaire administered at two hospitals in London. The seventy-four participants were aged over sixty-five.

Rebekah Schiff et al., *British Medical Journal*, June 17, 2000.

die naturally, not because the respirator was turned off." We forget that respirators are artificial. Feeding tubes are artificial. The most natural thing in the world is nature taking its course. Your proxy does not decide your death—*you* do. Your proxy only performs an act of love and mercy by ensuring that your wishes are respected.

Make sure your proxy has a copy of your Advanced Directives, and also give a copy to your doctor to place in your chart when you go to the hospital. Let your family know where they can find it quickly and easily. Bring your family together for a discussion early on in the disease process, or before you even get sick. Show them your Advanced Directives, let them hear your wishes clearly, and discuss their concerns. Discuss them now rather than over your hospital bed. It will be too late when you are in a coma, at which point *any* relative may insist that you be kept alive, and the doctors will have to keep the machines on. Afraid of being sued, the doctors will err on the side of doing too much rather than too little.

Doctors and Advanced Directives

A doctor may want you to stay "alive" because he'll feel he's failed if you die. Doctors may have been taught to fight to the bitter end, and they never have thought of death as the miracle that ends life, just as birth is the miracle that begins it. They may have been taught not to take verbal directives from an emotionally distraught relative. (Although who wouldn't be upset when a loved one is about to die?) They're worried about being hit with malpractice suits if they don't do everything conceivable to keep patients alive. And they don't want to get caught up in legal battles between family members. If even one relative says "keep him alive," doctors will follow the path of least legal danger and do so. Even a distant relative you haven't seen in twenty years can march into the hospital and tell the doctors to do everything possible to keep you alive. . . .

If you and your doctor or loved one's doctor do not see eye to eye, it is appropriate to ask for another physician. It is your right. You can ask the nurses for recommendations or you can call the hospital administrator.

The care most people receive reflects their doctors' beliefs and values. It is crucial to establish a relationship with a physician who shares your values and beliefs. When we are treated by physicians whose values differ from ours, we're often talked into taking more or less aggressive measures than we would like to. It is vital to make your wishes known in Advanced Directives and to appoint a strong advocate to watch over you. Otherwise, you may find your control over the circumstances of your death slipping away from you.

"[Advance directives] deny [the] reality of dying."

Advance Directives Fail to Give Dying Patients Control over Treatment

Peter G. Filene

One type of advance directive is the living will, a legal document that describes the treatments that doctors and family members should or should not administer if a person becomes incapacitated by terminal illness or enters a coma. Other types of advance directives include do-not-resuscitate (DNR) orders and the durable power of attorney for health care. In the following viewpoint, Peter G. Filene maintains that advance directives are ineffective because no one can predict what course of treatment will be desirable months or years prior to becoming ill. He asserts that advance directives encourage the myth that terminally ill patients can exercise control over their deaths. Filene is the author of *In the Arms of Others: A Cultural History of the Right-to-Die in America* and a professor of history at the University of North Carolina, Chapel Hill.

As you read, consider the following questions:
1. As cited by the author, what percentage of patients on life support had not written a living will?
2. How have patients and doctors joined together in a "dance of denial" over their control of death, in Filene's opinion?
3. According to the author, why does filling out an advance directive promote a false sense of "autonomy" or self-determination?

Nearly nine of ten people told pollsters that if they were on life-support with no hope of recovery, they would choose to withdraw treatment and die. In the same spirit, three of four said they would like to have a living will. Yet only 10 to 20 percent in the mid-1990s had actually written one. Whatever they believed in theory, in practice they didn't sit down and face the stark reality that might eventually befall them. Even when that reality arrived, an astounding number of people managed to look the other way. According to an American Medical Association (AMA) survey of patients *on life-support*, 85 percent still had not written a living will. In fact, 44 percent had not even told family members what they wished done if they suffered an irreversible coma. Doctors deserved to be faulted for ignoring patients' preferences, but all too often their patients had failed to define their preferences. The Patient Self-Determination Act ordered hospital staff to change their paternalistic behavior, but patients continued to shirk self-determination. Despite all the seminars, best-selling books, and television documentaries on "dying with dignity," despite the haunting presence of Karen Ann Quinlan, most Americans didn't write advance directives.

Advance Directives: Built-In Limitations

Patients blame doctors, doctors blame patients, and one can also blame the living will itself. The well-known bioethicist and gerontologist Joanne Lynn, for example, created a stir in 1991 with her article "Why I Don't Have a Living Will." Although she supported the Patient Self-Determination Act and encouraged her patients to establish advance directives, she hadn't written one for herself. She wasn't inefficient or imprudent, she said. Rather, "I fear that the effects of having one would be worse, in my situation, than not having one." The standard living will, she explained, fosters the belief that one won't be kept alive like Karen Ann Quinlan or Claire Conroy. But in fact it only protects persons who, with or without treatment, will die soon. Even if one adds clauses to anticipate dreaded contingencies, no one—especially not a layperson—can foretell what will turn out to be desirable or feasible when illness strikes. A respirator for a week or ten days or not at all? CPR [cardiopulmonary resuscitation] once, twice, as often as needed? A feeding tube? Rather than write a self-delusory script of her future, Lynn gave control to her husband. She signed a durable power of attorney, which named him as surrogate. And if she were to become incompetent, it asked doctors and judges to defer to his judgment.

Professional arrogance, personal weakness, and the limitations built into advance directives—each of these explains in part the shortcomings of the right-to-die policy. But only in part. Ultimately we need to recognize that all of them reflect the influence of two American values: abundance and individualism. In other words, how we die, or hope to die, is a cultural construction.

Medical Abundance

Patients and doctors have joined together in a dance of denial, clinging to the last spasms of life, neither of them wanting to be the first to admit that it would be better to stop. Another round of chemo [chemotherapy]. CPR. Give heroic treatment to the heroic fighter and never say die. When framed in these terms, anxiety about death becomes a kind of reckless faith, as if there will be more time, more happiness, more reason to hope. It's a medical version of the economic abundance that Americans after 1945 enjoyed and took for granted. The Presidential Commission for the Study of Ethical Problems in Medicine, for example, asserted in 1983 that, unlike other societies, the United States could use life-sustaining treatment without worrying about the price.

But by then that sort of affluent attitude was in fact misguided. Starting in the early 1970s, personal income for all but the wealthiest households leveled off. Unemployment spread across the manufacturing sector and "downsizing" across the white-collar sector. Instead of abundance, Americans began hearing about limits. In "the new constraint environment," one economist said, resources—including health resources—had to be rationed. "It is clear," one political scientist advised in 1988, "that we must . . . regulate our overindulgence of medical care for the individual. . . ." A 1996 television documentary on "Who Plays God?" didn't follow the usual plot line of whether patients should forgo

Kauffmann. © 1992 by Joel Kauffmann. Reprinted with permission.

life-support and whether doctors should comply. This time the plot wasn't bioethical but economic. "How do we decide when enough is enough?" asked the program host, George Strait. "And how much care can we really afford?"

The Weakness of Self-Determination

Americans aren't ready to accept that stricture—or if at all, they accept it for the society as a whole, not for themselves. Here is the second cultural value underlying the right-to-die policy and the second weakness: self-determination. When asked by Gallup pollsters in 1982 to rate a list of values, six of ten Americans gave "freedom to choose" the highest possible rating, while another 36 percent put it among the top five, ahead of "following God's will" and a "sense of accomplishment." This principle has been a mainstay of the American belief system for more than a century and a half, so entrenched (at least for men) that it has seemed to be an unquestionable truth. "This is a country of *self-made men*," Calvin Colton, a minister and Whig party pamphleteer, declared in 1844, "than which nothing better could be said of any state of society." Those rare men who went from log cabin to White House or rags to riches perpetuated the cultural myth. Nevertheless, when nineteenth-century Americans reached the end of life, they acknowledged the boundary of self-determination and entrusted themselves to the will of God. By the late twentieth century, medical treatment had changed and so had the sense of boundary. Doctors can push back death by means of technological "miracles," such as the respirator, organ transplants, and CPR. Modern Americans, in turn, presume they can determine their dying.

When a person fills out an advance directive, he is predicting—months or years ahead of a life-threatening illness—which medical treatments he will want, under which circumstances, and for how long. Bioethicists call this a claim to "autonomy" or self-determination, which has a comforting sound. An individual is choosing his course of action, free from constraint by others and in accordance with his personal values. Just beneath the surface, however, we should hear the desperate desire to control. The "director" is trying to exert control over how doctors and family treat him when he is helpless. The desperation reflects, in turn, the wishfulness of this process. The author of a living will is writing the last chapter of his autobiography before the intervening chapters have taken place. In contrast to those Victorian deathbed scenes of suffering and resignation, this modern chapter itemizes a painless, "dignified" scenario. Beneath the legal surface lurks fiction.

Denying the Reality of Death

Self-determination is a fiction not only in advance of dying but even more so in the midst of dying. The principle of autonomy makes sense in the case of a pregnant woman demanding the right to abortion, for example, or a patient claiming the right to a candid diagnosis. When it comes to terminal illness, an individual's right has a very different meaning—or possibly no meaning. For existential freedom stops at the door of death; at best we can exercise autonomy up to the threshold. But modern medicine has made the width of that threshold uncertain. In Joanne Lynn's graphic phrase, "People really die now by inches more than miles," and along the way we will become less and less competent. Like Claire Conroy, we may remain conscious but unable to ask for an end to unendurable pain. Or like Karen Ann Quinlan and as many as 35,000 others now, we may be freed from pain but sentenced to survival. Our fate will rest in the hands of others. By pledging exclusive allegiance to "autonomy," we deny this reality of dying and feed the very dread we're trying to overcome. No wonder so few people have written a living will.

Periodical Bibliography

The following articles have been selected to supplement the diverse views presented in this chapter.

Burke J. Balch	"Terminally Ill Often Change Their Minds About Will to Live, Study Shows," *National Right to Life News*, September 14, 1999.
Greg Borzo	"In Short Order," *American Medical News*, May 24–31, 1999.
Richard Burnham	"Hospice Care: Making an Informed Choice," *USA Today Magazine*, March 1999.
Business Week	"Giving More Patients 'A Good Death,'" November 20, 2000.
Christina Walker Campi	"When Dying Is as Hard as Birth," *New York Times*, January 5, 1998.
Thomas R. Cole	"We Have a Sacred Covenant with the Dead," *Los Angeles Times*, March 8, 2002.
Thomas E. Finucane	"How Gravely Ill Becomes Dying: A Key to End-of-Life Care," *JAMA*, November 3, 1999.
Sharon I. Fraser and James W. Walters	"Death—Whose Decision? Euthanasia and the Terminally Ill," *Journal of Medical Ethics*, April 2000.
Judith Graham	"Shorter Time in Hospice Care Cheats the Dying, Say Agencies," *Seattle Times*, June 6, 1999.
August Gribbin	"Graceful Exit," *Washington Times*, January 7, 2001.
Jennifer G. Hickey	"A Safe Haven for the Dying?" *Insight on the News*, January 25, 1999.
Gina Kolata	"Living Wills Are Rarely of Aid, Study Says," *New York Times*, April 8, 1997.
Maria LaGanga	"Trying to Figure the Beginning of the End," *Los Angeles Times*, October 15, 1999.
Charlotte Lobuono	"A Detailed Examination of Advance Directives," *Patient Care*, November 15, 2000.
Carol M. Ostrum	"Caregivers Torn over Oregon's Suicide Law," *Seattle Times*, March 20, 2000.
Wesley J. Smith	"Our Discardable People," *Human Life Review*, Summer 1998.
Sheryl Gay Stolberg	"Doctors Walk Fine Line in Giving Painkillers to Dying Patients," *San Diego Union-Tribune*, October 21, 1998.
Don Udall	"When Someone Is Alive, but Not Living," *Newsweek*, June 14, 1999.

How Can People Cope with Death?

Chapter Preface

The way people have coped with the inevitability of death has undergone dramatic shifts throughout the course of history. Donald Heinz, in his book *The Last Passage: Recovering a Death of Our Own*, describes how in the fifteenth century, people attempted to master the "art of dying" through the use of death manuals, which "took their place alongside books on the proper way of manipulating a table knife, conducting a conversation, . . . and playing chess." Indeed, death was viewed as a force that one could prepare for. Later, in the nineteenth century, "the relation of the dying person to the family came into focus." Most people died at home surrounded by friends and family members, a regular occurrence in those times since infectious disease claimed many young lives.

By the middle of the twentieth century, however, death in America had evolved into a force to be assiduously avoided by means of hospitals, medical technology, and a culture of denial. Death moved out of the home and became institutionalized—close to three-quarters of American deaths now take place in hospitals and nursing homes. Richard John Neuhaus, the editor of *First Things* magazine, notes that, "as children of a culture radically, even religiously, devoted to youth and health, many find it incomprehensible, indeed offensive, that the word 'good' should in any way be associated with death. Death, it is thought, is an unmitigated evil, the very antithesis of all that is good." Dissatisfied with its institutionalization, some observers contend that Americans must return to a more natural conception of death. Not only will this help people cope with the prospect of their own deaths, but, the reasoning goes, it will better enable people to handle grief after a loved one dies.

One area where natural death proponents are pushing for change is the American funeral. Reformers view the traditional funeral and its accompanying mourning rituals as an empty ceremony that puts all the responsibility for care of the dying into the hands of strangers, most likely funeral directors and religious figures. They want the funeral ceremony returned to the home and to involve the active participation of family and friends. Explains the Final Passages organization, which advocates home and family-directed funerals, "In a home funeral, family and friends may begin by ceremoniously washing the body and dressing them in garments that honor their unique personality. . . . A home funeral provides a safe, loving and appropriate place where one can discuss life and death and express emotions of grief and loss. Decorating a wooden or cardboard casket may give those who are having difficulty expressing these feelings a creative and healing outlet." Supporters maintain that this hands-on approach will encourage more reflection on the meaning of death and ease the pain of grief and loss.

There is a lively debate over how people can best cope with death and grief, from conducting mourning rituals to seeking out mental health professionals to embracing spirituality. Not surprisingly, some observers disagree that abandoning traditional funerals is beneficial to the bereaved. The fact that there is such a debate, however, indicates that once again, society is rethinking its conception of death. In the following chapter, experts and laypersons share their views on ways to cope with death and grief.

> *"Spiritual support is essential in the care of the dying. We need to help foster hope, love, and contentment with their lives in the final days of living."*

The Dying Must Make Spiritual Peace with Death

M. Christina Puchalski

M. Christina Puchalski is assistant professor of internal medicine at the Center to Improve Care of the Dying at the George Washington University School of Medicine. She maintains in the following viewpoint that supporting the spiritual needs of dying patients is more effective in helping them cope with death than encouraging a fight to the end with aggressive medical treatment. In Puchalski's opinion, the dying need an opportunity to bring closure to their lives by forgiving those they had conflicts with, making peace with themselves and God, and saying good-bye to friends and family.

As you read, consider the following questions:
1. According to the author, why are spiritual concerns so important for dying patients?
2. Why shouldn't all medical cases be treated aggressively, in Puchalski's opinion?
3. As recounted by the author, how did Peter Roberts's embrace of spirituality allow him to make peace with death?

From "Facing Death with True Dignity," by M. Christina Puchalski, *World and I*, July 1998. Copyright © 1998 by News World Communications, Inc. Reprinted with permission.

Jim is a 35-year-old gentleman with AIDS. He has two children with whom he is very close. He is dying. Jim called me the other day because he said he felt death was coming soon. He knew that because his frail body no longer carries his clothes the way it used to. He almost did not recognize the face he tried to shave each morning. The sunken eyes lacked that sparkle of life as they peeked out beyond the prominent bony orbits. Every step has been an enormous effort and every breath a labored exhalation.

"I am not who I used to be," he said. "My children clean the house, cook the meals, and nurse me. They are just kids, and I can't be a parent anymore. I have no energy to give. My son is angry at me because he thinks I have given up. I don't think so. I just think it is my time to go."

As I listened to Jim's feelings, his anxieties about leaving the people he loves, mixed with fleeting seconds of peaceful resolve that this is the way of nature, the way of God, I couldn't help but wonder was there one more fight Jim could win with his illness? Was his son right? Could I encourage him to hang on for just a few more months?

Supporting Spirituality

One key concern of dying patients that needs to be supported is their spirituality. The need for attentiveness to the spiritual concerns of patients has been recognized by many authors. The term spirituality has been used in different ways by different authors. A broad, inclusive definition: Spirituality is that which gives meaning to one's life and draws one to transcend oneself.

Spirituality is a broader concept than religion, although that is one expression of spirituality. Other expressions include prayer, meditation, interactions with others or nature, and relationship with God or a higher power. Spirituality has been cited as integral to the dying person's achievement of the developmental task of transcendence and important for health-care providers to recognize and foster. According to Sally Leighton, writing in "When Mortality Calls, Don't Hang Up," "The physician will do better to be close by to tune in carefully on what may be transpiring spiritually, both in order to comfort the dying and to broaden his or her own understanding of life at its ending."

Some spiritual questions confront each dying person. Is there purpose to his life as he suffers, and can he transcend his suffering and see something or someone beyond that? Is he at peace, hopeful, or in despair? What nourishes his personal sense of value: prayer, religious commitment, personal faith, relationship with others? Do his beliefs help him cope with anxiety about death, pain, and achieving peace?

Saint Therese of Lisieux, a nineteenth-century Carmelite nun, observed of the sisters in her community whose deaths she had witnessed:

> It was without effort that the dying passed on to a better life, and immediately after their death an expression of joy and peace covered their faces and gave the impression almost that they were only asleep. Surely this was true because, after the image of the world has passed away, they will awaken to enjoy eternally the delights.

Therese and her sisters had a profound faith in God and the afterlife. They nourished this faith with prayer. Death was a transition to union with God; as their time drew near, they prepared for it spiritually and hence died in peace. She also had the insight to think about death early in life: "The friends we had there were too worldly; they knew too well how to ally the joys of this earth. . . . They didn't think about death enough, and yet death had paid its visit to a great number of those whom I knew, the young, the rich, the happy!"

Fighting Death Increases Suffering

What a contrast to our present society. We focus on youth, on looking young, acting young, having aggressive medical treatment to the very last possible moment. Only in the last days of life do we think about the possibility of death. Advances in technology have enabled us to prolong and extend life.

Not all cases should be treated aggressively, however. There comes a time in the course of any illness when cure is no longer an option. In many cases, the techniques used to prolong life actually prolong the dying process, often with increased suffering or loss of dignity.

The SUPPORT study, conducted by five major medical centers, showed that the majority of U.S. deaths are in hospital settings with frequent use of ventilator support, artificial feedings, and inadequate pain control and anxiety management.

In encouraging people to fight to the end, we neglect to give them the opportunity to bring closure to their lives; to complete unfinished goals; to forgive those they had conflicts with, to be forgiven; to make peace with themselves, with God; to say good-bye; and to die with dignity.

Feeding the Hunger for Inner Peace

Death is not an event but a process, a process with which we should all energetically engage as soon as we are genuinely aware of our own mortality. We all know that moment: it is that time in our lives when we stop looking forward and instead start calculating how much time we have left. It is a sobering discovery. The end of youth.

The argument continues that as we face the last few months or days of life we do not regret any material or social shortcomings nor, indeed, underachievement. We don't regret failing to make millions, get a knighthood, or become prime minister; or, at least, any such regrets are passing musings. But we hunger for inner peace, and the central impediment to that peace is our failure to be reconciled with others: past wives or lovers, estranged children, other members of our family, colleagues and friends. Peace is only possible if we make those relationships whole.

Peter Chadlington, *Spectator*, July 31, 1999.

I was honored to be able to walk the journey with Father Peter Roberts, a Carmelite priest, as he prepared for his death. Pete had metastatic pancreatic cancer. As we talked about cancer and death, his hand trembled in mine, his voice quivered as he held back tears; he was afraid. His will to continue living was so strong, he grasped for any miraculous explanation that could fulfill his will.

Yet deep within, he understood that it was God's will, not his, that would prevail. Pete's life had not been easy. He faced many challenges that often weighed him down and made it difficult to go on. The turning point for him came when he acknowledged his alcoholism and sought help with the support of his community.

He learned that he was powerless, which was not an admission of defeat but a giving up of the illusion of self sufficiency. He often said, "God's will, not mine, that is why I am sober and alive today." And so, 25 years later, when he faced the greatest challenge any of us will ever face, he simply turned to God and asked for His help and accepted what God had in store for him.

A few days after our initial conversation regarding his diagnosis, Pete let me know he had decided not to have any chemotherapy. Laughing, he said, "I don't have a wife to go home and vomit for, so I'll just take whatever happens." Underneath that surface humor he so often exhibited was a gentle resolve to accept his dying. This is not to say that once he had made this decision it was instantly a peaceful one.

The first two months were filled with anxieties about dying: Will there be intolerable pain? Would he suffocate? Will he be so helpless that he won't be able to take care of his basic necessities? His theology was challenged. The rigors of adherence to rules were his way of life for 70 years. Now, some of those rules frightened him. Would he go to hell? Had he lived a good enough life as a Christian, a priest, and a brother, as a son and a friend? The judgmental God who had held him in check most of his life and, to some degree, brought him security was closer at hand.

Making Peace with God

Pete was scared. Was this the God he had relied on all his sober life—the forgiving God, the loving God? That God was harder for Pete to understand. What about his friends, family, and community: Would old squabbles be forgotten and old hurts be mended? Pete sat and cried as he spoke of several men in the religious community to whom he felt especially close.

Could he let go? Would he miss them so much that he would hold on longer? Would he really be missed after he died? Would he be remembered? How? I too was scared. I felt the pang of impending separation and wondered if I would be able to handle his permanent physical absence. I was used to his jokes and words of encouragement when I had difficult days. I looked forward to his sermons, because I knew he would make me laugh and remember to take myself a little less seriously. And laughter is healing.

There wasn't a conversation we had, even in the midst of his suffering at the end, where we didn't share at least a few moments of humor. That was what kept Pete going. Pete had also lived his whole life preparing for his eventual death and meeting God, so this time was not a shock but a conclusion to a life's journey.

My own acceptance of his eventual death came when he gave me his books, all inscribed carefully in multicolored ink. (Pete underlined passages of his books in different-colored ink for emphasis as he was learning.) Initially, I regarded the books as a loan; it was easier at some level to pretend that he might recover. Each day, I'd glance at his books on my bookshelf and gradually accepted that he would die soon.

Pete's initial struggle with sadness and anxiety gradually gave way to increasing inner peace and contentment. Pete had decided to make his last months on earth his "final helpout" as he called it. "I want to show the men in my community, my family and friends, how to die well." He wanted to let us see that it wasn't something to dread and fear but rather something to look forward to at a deep spiritual level.

While often he felt a profound sadness and anxiety about leaving, he never forgot about being a presence of gratitude to those around him. One day, a few weeks before he died, I walked into his room, a simple one with minimal amenities. He sat up in bed, gaunt, panting with each breath. Such penetrating sadness came over me; he looked so frail, both weak and in pain. He looked up at me and said, "I am so grateful. I have a wonderful community, family, and friends who have all been so good to me. What a blessed life I have had! I am so grateful for it all."

From behind the ashen skin and tired, drawn eyes came a radiance of joy and peace. There was physical pain and disability, but Pete had transcended that. He had put to rest all the conflicts of his past and all his insecurities and fears. The judgmental God was no longer in center stage. He truly saw God's goodness and grace in all around him and felt at peace in letting go.

His final day on earth was a miraculous one. He was surrounded by the men of his community, by his brother Bill, his sister Polly, and me. We held him, propped up pillows for him, gave him medication to relieve his pain, and prayed with him. His spirit gradually left amid singing and praying and love. We chanted the song "Jesus, Remember Me When We Come Into Your Kingdom" as Pete died. There was no suffering, no pain, no suffocation. Pete died in peace. And as Saint Therese had noticed of her sisters' deaths, with a look of joy and contentment.

What the Dying Need

People who are dying need time to make peace not only with death but also with life. And those of us who are not imminently dying need to face the possibilities of our eventual deaths and live life accordingly. Wayne Muller says in Touching the Divine:

> There are times in all of our lives when we are forced to reach deep into ourselves to feel the truth of our real nature. For each of us there comes a moment when we can no longer live our lives by accident. Life throws us into questions that some of us refuse to ask until we are confronted by death or some tragedy in our lives. What do I know to be most deeply true? What do I love and have I loved well? Who do I believe myself to be and what have I placed on the center of the altar of my life? Where do I belong? What will people find in the ashes of my incarnation when this is all over? How shall I live my life knowing that I will die? And what is my gift to the family of the earth?

Remembering, assessing, searching for meaning, forgiving, reconciling, loving, and hoping are all part of the spiritual journey especially active during the time of dying. It is critical that we allow people who are dying the time to go through this important journey.

Spiritual support is essential in the care of the dying. We need to help foster hope, love, and contentment with their lives in the final days of living. We need to provide an environment where people can be still, pray, laugh, cry, hold, and be held as they are dying.

I don't think I will try to coach Jim on for another win with his illness. I will hold his hand, listen to his fears, his hopes and beliefs, give him the time to bring closure to his life, listen to his stories from the past and dreams for his children after he is gone. And I will support him as he gets ready to die.

> "*There are still a few of us left who think that dying . . . stinks, and that there really is no effective way to do it well.*"

The Dying Have the Right to Die Angry

Marshall B. Kapp

In the following viewpoint, Marshall B. Kapp asserts that encouraging dying patients to embrace death as an opportunity for personal growth does not necessarily enable them to better cope with death. According to Kapp, patients should be allowed to remain true to their personalities, even if that results in bitterness and resistance to the dying process. Insisting that patients become receptive of professional efforts to foster growth, forgiveness, and personal fulfillment at the end of life may cause feelings of shame and guilt in some patients. Kapp is a professor of community health and psychiatry at Wright State University School of Medicine in Dayton, Ohio.

As you read, consider the following questions:

1. According to the author, what factors signify a "successfully" managed death under the ethically correct dogma promoted by health care professionals?
2. How would Kapp's personal reaction to a diagnosis of terminal illness likely contrast with the death-as-a-time-of-personal-growth movement?
3. What constitutes "successful dying," in Kapp's opinion?

From "The Right to Die Mad," by Marshall B. Kapp, *The Pharos*, Winter 2000. Copyright © 2000 by Marshall B. Kapp. Reprinted with permission.

In American bioethics circles at the turn of the millennium, the manner in which most people now die is one of the foremost "in" subjects of critical attention.

Attention on the Dying

- The prestigious Institute of Medicine recently released a report lambasting the medical care establishment and its key participants (including but not limited to physicians) for their many current deficiencies in dealing with dying patients sensitively and effectively.
- Major funding sources have initiated massive campaigns, exemplified by the Robert Wood Johnson Foundation's Last Acts initiative, the Education for Physicians on End of Life Care (EPEC) project jointly initiated by the Robert Wood Johnson Foundation and the American Medical Association, and the Open Society Institute's Project on Death in America, to address these serious shortcomings by sponsoring relevant research projects, improved professional and public education on these matters, and political advocacy.
- New organizations such as Americans for Better Care of the Dying have sprouted up for the express purpose of vigorously pushing these agenda items.
- Legal scholars and associations are actively promoting legislative, regulatory, and administrative practice reforms in areas such as pain management.
- Journals in medicine, bioethics, and health policy are teeming with articles directed toward physicians and other health care professionals, admonishing them to do a much better job of caring, and especially of the nontechnological aspects of caring, for patients as they approach the ends of their earthly lives.
- A spate of moving, often almost poetic, books have been published in the past few years by physicians, family members, and others describing both positive and awful first-hand experiences with dying patients and extrapolating from those experiences important insights and lessons for the medical care system and the larger society.

The general thrust of these shared insights is to the effect that, in the overwhelming majority of contemporary circumstances, the process of each patient's dying can, and ought to, be "successfully" managed, just as with virtually every other facet of life. Under the emerging ethically correct dogma, success in choreographing the dying process is signified by supporting the patient, family, and friends in the waning days (or weeks or months) of life in ways that enable the patient to die "well," finding meaning, peace, joy, growth, and fulfillment—even "new beginnings"—in his or her life as the moment of departure inevitably arrives. In this "good death"-with-dignity paradigm, empathetic, respectful end-of-life care empowers the patient to bring positive closure to previously unresolved, nettling issues and controversies, to die with no unnecessarily unfinished personal business, regrets, or animosities.

Underlying the achievement of these laudatory goals at the micro, or individual bedside level is the presumption that, at the macro level, American society must replace its prevailing death-denying mind-set with one that accepts, and to a large extent welcomes, the mortality of its individual members. Death, it is claimed, must be envisioned as a necessary, wholesome part of nature to be willingly anticipated rather than as a foreign enemy to be feared and loathed. Only with this quantum change in social attitudes will our medical care system move away from routine but futile technological assaults on dying patients that only prolong an undignified and often painful dying process, and substitute instead a supportive and empowering environment that looks with favor on the inevitable end and tries to make the most of this (quite literally) once-in-a-lifetime opportunity.

It is difficult (even for me, an attorney trained to argue about everything) to quarrel with these noble and overdue sentiments. Certainly, neither as individuals nor as a society can we deny the finality of human mortality, although much of our religious energy is aimed at trying desperately to do exactly that. Surely, alleviating physical and emotional pain near the end of life (or at any other time, for that matter) is an objective to be pursued resolutely through whatever pharmacologic or other means are needed. No reasonable person would argue with calls for greater sensitivity, compassion, and understanding in caring for the dying. Similarly, in contrast to much of current medical practice, physicians and other health professionals unquestionably must perform much better in terms of honoring patients' autonomous medical treatment and nontreatment preferences.

The Right to Die Mad

While all of these objectives should be endorsed and implemented enthusiastically, one word of caution is nevertheless appropriate. Not to be a (no pun intended) killjoy, but there are still a few of us left who think that dying—both the ultimate outcome and the process leading to and culminating in that outcome—stinks, and that there really is no effective way to do it well.

Kauffmann. © 1992 by Joel Kauffmann. Reprinted with permission.

I do not know (and no person can truly predict for himself in the abstract) how I would react to being told that I had a diagnosis of a terminal illness. I suspect, however, that my reaction might not make Elisabeth Kübler-Ross or today's proponents of the death-as-a-time-of-personal-growth movement very proud. Indeed, I might confidently surmise that my reaction to the bad news would be one of anger, frustration, terror, and bitter feelings of injustice, and that these sentiments would intensify rather than mellow as the dying process proceeded. I might not want to tell those with whom I had conflicts that, in the end, I forgive and love them: I might, in fact, want to tell some people whom I didn't like what I honestly thought of them. If my prognostication is accurate, then, facilitating an autonomous, authentic end to my life ought to entail others respecting my right to die mad, with a frown instead of a smile.

My point is not at all to disparage sincere and well-intentioned efforts to make the dying process a more positive experience for those patients and their families (and there will be many of them) who are amenable to, indeed thankfully receptive of, this approach. My caveat, though, is that a personally defined successful dying may take many forms, and that those patients who choose to resist professional efforts to implore growth, forgiveness, and personal fulfillment at the end of life should not be labeled—before or after death—as failures. Allowing and helping a patient to remain true to individual character and personality to the very end—even if that entails bitterness and anger—is preferable to an uninvited interdisciplinary team of health care professionals energetically hectoring the dying patient to change personalities at that late date and making the patient feel additional guilt and shame for resisting the thanatologically sensitive experts' injunctions to "Have a nice death."

Rejecting "Positive Growth"

Some commentators have called for the development of quality assurance standards against which particular health plans and health care providers could be evaluated regarding the totality of care for patients engaged in the dying process, and have suggested making these evaluation results available to the consumer public. Such innovation could substantially improve end-of-life care in the United States if it encourages and assists providers to make accessible to desirous patients supportive forms of care to help those patients progress through the dying process in an atmosphere of human compassion, kindness, and love. Positive growth at the end of life, however, should not be forced paternalistically on an unwilling patient, any more than an unwanted feeding tube or respirator. Neither patients nor providers should be penalized or stigmatized when patients reject the opportunity to die with equanimity and without a fuss. Successful dying means I have the right to die mad, if that turns out to be the final chapter of my life's story and I choose to stick to it.

> *"At [nontraditional funeral] gatherings we discovered that our fear of death and the unknown had diminished tremendously."*

Nontraditional Funerals Help the Bereaved Cope with Death

Jerri Lyons

Increasingly, people are requesting that do-it-yourself home funerals be conducted when they die in place of traditional funeral services. Home funerals rely on the participation of family members and friends to prepare the body for burial or cremation and to conduct a ceremony based on the instructions of the deceased. Jerri Lyons contends in the following viewpoint that by taking on responsibility for the care of their loved ones, home-funeral participants can reduce their fear of death and more readily come to terms with their loss. The author is the founder and codirector of the Natural Death Care Project and director of the Home Funeral Ministry, organizations that help people create home funerals.

As you read, consider the following questions:

1. How did handling Carolyn's dead body provide Lyons with a sense of the reality of her friend's death?
2. As stated by the author, what is one of the goals of the Natural Death Care Project?
3. How much less does a home funeral cost compared to a traditional embalming, viewing, and burial, according to Lyons?

Excerpted from "The Natural Death Care Project & Home Funeral Ministry: Two Projects Whose Time Has Come—An Interview with Jerri Lyons," *Grace Millennium*, Winter 2000. Copyright © 2000 by *Grace Millennium*. Reprinted with permission.

What inspired me to begin this project was the unexpected death of my friend Carolyn. I had no idea, when she went to work one morning to take care of an elder in her eighties, that she herself would be making her own transition. She began her day feeling great, but after breakfast she started having trouble breathing. Marie, the elder woman she was looking after, called 911. The ambulance came, but they couldn't resuscitate her.

Instructions for a Home Funeral

Carolyn had gone to sit on the porch and get some air. Marie saw her roll over on the lawn with a smile on her face, and that was it. She was only fifty-six years old, and was as alive as we are right now. She was quite an active and gregarious person, and her death was a shock to her friends and family. The evening of the day she died, we discovered that several years earlier she had prepared a set of detailed instructions about what she wanted at the time of her death. She had given these instructions to her friend Norma.

When Norma's husband died, no one knew what he wanted—burial, cremation, what kind of ceremony. That inspired Carolyn to get a group of friends together one day to sit down and write out instructions that included what flowers they wanted, the music to be played, what they would like on an altar, and so forth. Carolyn wrote that she did not want to be embalmed, she did not want an autopsy, and she did not want to be turned over to a mortuary. She wanted to be brought home by her friends, to have her body dressed and bathed at home and to be transported to the crematorium by her friends. She had told Norma, "It's a good thing you have a van. You can use it to transport my body." Norma said, "Don't be ridiculous. I probably won't even own this van when you die." Sure enough, several months later, Carolyn did die, and Norma's van was used to transport her body home from the hospital and to the crematorium. . . .

I was profoundly moved by the three days of personal care given to Carolyn following her death, including the experience of bringing her body home in a body bag, and unzipping it to find her looking as beautiful and peaceful as a baby. In touching her, I was able to get a sense of the reality of her death. I had not seen her at the hospital, so touching her body helped me begin to integrate in my own body, with my own senses, that she really had departed. Her bathing and dressing was so consciously and conscientiously done. It felt like a ritual—a very ancient rite of passage. Four of us women participated in that ceremony and we occasionally spoke to Carolyn, somehow feeling that she was there and could hear us.

"Time Out of Time"

At these ritual times, you are already in another state of mind—I call it "time out of time." There is so much going on, on other energy levels. There is a sense of spiritual intervention, angelic presence, and a special quality of heart-opening and bonding. You are doing something very meaningful and authentic. We had formed a phone tree, so after the preparation of the body many people came over and visited Carolyn, each in their own way—some silently, some singing, some chanting, some reading. Every one entered her house with the same sense of disbelief, trying to find answers for why this had happened. Carolyn was lying on a futon in a room that we had prepared and made sacred to honor her.

In the evening, we had a formal ceremony. We brought her body into the living room, brightly lit with candles and filled with flowers and fragrances. We surrounded her with our love, prayers and meditations. Carolyn's body was taken to the crematorium the next day. I hadn't expected to stay with the group the whole way through, but I kept feeling called back. Things that I was supposed to do fell away—in the synchronistic way that things seem to fall into place during important times. I was able to continue participating; I helped take her to the crematorium, and joined in a meal afterwards.

From Grief to Joy

A full spectrum of emotions can follow a person's death. I experienced waves of grief from the depths of my soul. Then, as a group, we would experience a joy and euphoric celebration. We wondered why we were experiencing such high feelings, yet we sensed Carolyn's presence in this very clearly. I felt as though she were orchestrating the whole thing. Even her sense of humor came through. When Norma and her friend Dana were preparing to take Carolyn's body to the crematorium, they found a piece of driftwood that fit the shape of her hand perfectly. Then they found a bird wing and placed it on her breast and a bowl of cookie fortunes, which they taped on her body. They asked, "Where should we put this one, Carolyn?" They read the fortune and said, "Oh, on your knee. Okay!" Then they taped it on. This was just like Carolyn. She laughed a lot and had a great sense of humor. That humorous aspect was not left out.

After her body was cremated, Carolyn's ashes were brought to her home. That happened to be our Reiki meeting night. Instead of doing Reiki, we had a special ceremony with her ashes, passing them around and placing them in small bags. She loved to travel, and one of her instructions was to scatter her ashes all over the world. We each took some in order to take them to special sacred places around the world.

We continued to meet weekly to plan Carolyn's memorial service, which occurred a month later on her birthday. At those gatherings we discovered that our fear of death and the unknown had diminished tremendously. Our experience with Carolyn had taken us through a doorway that I think most people in this country have not accessed. This is because most of our society has delegated death to institutions and industry, instead of taking on the responsibility of caring for our loved ones.

Carolyn's personality definitely came through during this whole event, and it was important to us to include her. Each segment of this journey was all about her, and each person's history with her. Together we designed a meaningful and unique send-off for our beloved friend.

Natural Death Care Project

A year and a half after Carolyn died, I decided that I wanted to start a project to help other people have a similarly wonderful experience. On December 10, 1995, I met with a group of friends who were also interested in this idea. Even though we didn't yet have a name or form, that was the birthing of the Natural Death Care Project.

After another year my friend Janelle, who had been working for Hospice, lost her aunt. She asked our project to assist her with the arrangements, and was particularly impressed by the results of this choice. She knew the loving care provided by Hospice, but also saw that when a person died, a funeral home was called and a transportation person would show up and whisk the body away with no time for family closure. The body was sometimes wrapped and the face covered without even asking the family whether that was acceptable. The body was not always handled with loving respect.

It turned out that Janelle's aunt had left her an inheritance, so she left her Hospice work to volunteer with our project. She became my co-director. Six months later, we became a program of the nonprofit Community Network for Appropriate Technologies (CNAT), which had been running for about twenty years in Sonoma County. One of its many programs, the Journey Project, includes a book called *Journey to Life's End*. The author, CNAT director Susan Keller, helps us prepare for a death by including information about filling out forms, and stories about seniors she personally cared for.

The Natural Death Care Project has also created classes and workshops to teach other people this work. One of our goals is to help other communities begin service organizations to guide people through home- or family-directed funerals. We offer in-services, presentations, consultations and four-hour classes with continuing education credits (CEUs) for professionals. . . .

Home Funeral Ministry

When the Natural Death Care Project became an educational program under CNAT, we split off our service work and started the Home Funeral Ministry to help families create home funerals. This service includes coaching people through bathing, dressing and preserving the body, having a wake and ceremony, helping them complete and file the paperwork, and accompanying them to the crematorium or cemetery of their choice. The cost is very reasonable—half to a third of what people generally pay.

The most basic cost for a standard institutional cremation (called direct cremation) is about $1300. This would
cover the removal of a body, paperwork and the cremation.
We can help families do this for less than half that cost.
Much of the savings comes from not using a mortuary or

Funeral Facts

Caring for your own dead is legal in most states. (Check with
your local Office of Vital Records or Lisa Carlson's book,
Caring for the Dead: Your Final Act of Love, Upper Access,
1987.)

Embalming is not essential. Dry ice works well for preservation during a three-day home ceremony.

The modern practice of embalming began during the Civil
War, for bodies shipped long distances. By 1920, almost all
bodies in the U.S. were embalmed. The practice is still rare
in other countries.

By 1900, both birth and death had been institutionalized in
the U.S., moved out of the home and into hospitals. In
March 1998, *U.S. News & World Report* estimated the average
cost of a funeral in the U.S. at $8,000.

Traditional funeral homes mark up the price of a casket by
300 to 500 percent. The rubber gasket on a protective casket
costs $8, but adds up to $800 to the price.

In a "sealed" casket, the body will not dehydrate naturally.
Instead it putrefies in an anaerobic environment. If the casket is closed too tightly, the gasses can't get out, and the casket explodes.

Casket plans for building a homemade wooden casket: $15.95.
For a cardboard cremation casket: $34.96 plus shipping. Con-
tact Natural Death Care Project (NDCP).

Corporate funeral chains are buying up local funeral homes
and cemeteries worldwide. Since there are far more mortuaries than can be supported by the death rate, the funeral industry depends on aggressive selling of expensive services.

In California, a family member or Durable Power of Attorney for Health Care (DPAHC) can 1) act in lieu of a funeral
director to orchestrate all arrangements and carry out all decisions; 2) fill out and file end-of-life documentation; 3)
transport deceased in any vehicle to a home, place of ceremony, crematory or cemetery.

Lisa Carlson, *Caring for the Dead*, 1998, and the National Death Care Project website: www.naturaldeathcare.org.

funeral home for arrangements. Mortuaries have a non-declinable overhead fee. This means that when you walk in the door, you are charged for staff and overhead. Everything else is extra. Most often people are in such an emotional state that they are not likely to make clear and wise choices. They may not even know what questions to ask, or what other options might be available. They are confused by a lot of information and often choose beyond their means. These choices might include a more expensive casket, embalming, viewing and preparation of the body, a chapel service, burial or scattering of ashes—all of which could push the price to several thousand dollars. The average burial cost in this country is about $8,000 to $10,000. Most of the families we help can do this for one-quarter to one-third that cost—depending on the cost of the casket and the cemetery they choose.

A service like Home Funeral Ministry is so much needed. We are not just supporting people in physically getting things done. We support them emotionally and spiritually as well, and hold the space for them to create what they want. This kind of reassurance allows a meaningful process to unfold in a natural way. Some people come into the experience frightened and nervous. Although we may have ancient memories in our cells of caring for our ancestors at death, we have no current pictures in our minds—no references, visual recordings or positive storytelling from our relatives to give us confidence.

Many families tell me that during the time surrounding a death, a lot of healing of old wounds occurs. People's hearts are so open that armor falls away and walls come down. This provides an opportunity for healing on many levels. It also bonds people that never knew each other. I feel bonded to all the families I have been through this with, and so far I have walked through about 120 family-directed funerals. This is very different from a funeral business with a funeral director who helps people with arrangements but separates himself from them. We are not working behind the scenes. We are with the family—like a *doula* or a midwife in birthing. We are right there, coaching them or participating with them in ceremonies. We become part of the family. One of the things that makes this work so rich is that we get to experience many different kinds of rituals. We support all cultures, religions and backgrounds. . . .

Creative Caskets

New businesses are sprouting up all over the country that provide options to expensive caskets. Kate Broderson has a business in Forestville called A Plain Pine Box. She very lovingly builds pine boxes using high-quality materials. Caskets are also being created using ecological materials such as straw.

Many people are choosing to paint and decorate the caskets themselves. You can get a cardboard casket after, or even before, someone dies, and decorate it in a most beautiful way. We have an entire slide show and photo album of such caskets. Each one could be in an art gallery. They are all about the person who died, and can take any creative direction—with writings, paintings, glitter, rainbow paper, flowers and so forth.

A box can be padded with batting or blankets, and covered with special material. Some people even make pillows to match. One woman, Michele, planning for her own home funeral, told her story, "A Death Without Fear," to the *Santa Rosa Press Democrat*. Her friend lined the casket with beautiful purple satin and painted Egyptian icons on top and around the inside of the casket. Michele followed an Egyptian religion, and her elaborate funeral ceremony in the "enchanted forest" behind their home in Guerneville included readings from *The Egyptian Book of the Dead*.

In some cases, people with a terminal illness decorate their own caskets. They can even have a living wake, in which they invite all their friends to a party—a healing celebration where everyone gets to speak their truth and say wonderful things before you die. I have attended several of these.

There is so much potential in this work. I am now learning about the use of essential oils in after-death care—how to anoint the body with oils to help with spiritual release and also to calm those who are grieving. . . .

There is a trend in our country toward new burial procedures and do-it-yourself funerals. We were mentioned in a *Life* magazine article, and we were contacted by *20-20*, which was looking to film a home funeral for use in a television segment. With this mainstream-oriented interest, I know that a big change is coming. Just like the home-birth movement, and the creation of birthing rooms in hospitals, I expect that home funerals and other new options will become normal options within my lifetime.

"Funerals are no longer somber rituals where we pay our respects to the dead. They are cabaret."

Nontraditional Funerals Do Not Help the Bereaved Cope with Death

Joe Queenan

In the following viewpoint, Joe Queenan argues that non-traditional funerals, which often feature popular music and comedic eulogies, are a shallow attempt to cover up the unpleasant reality of death with a personalized, party-like atmosphere and provide little solace to the bereaved. Nontraditional funerals have grown in popularity as the post–World War II baby boom generation has entered the stages of late middle age. The devolution of funerals from somber grief rituals that pay respect to the dead to foolish "fun-fests" demonstrates how uncomfortable many Americans are with the process of death and dying, in Queenan's opinion. The author is a contributing writer at *GQ* magazine.

As you read, consider the following questions:
1. According to Queenan, what are some of the characteristics of nontraditional funerals?
2. Why don't baby boomers like somber funeral services, in Queenan's opinion?
3. In the author's opinion, how does the statement of Julius Erving following the death of his son demonstrate his discomfort with the language of grief?

In 1987, after a good friend died a particularly hideous death, I wrote an op-ed piece in the *New York Times* complaining about his funeral service. This is the way Baby Boomers process grief; they write op-ed pieces or, worse, read them. In the article, I chided the local priest for knowing so little about my friend's background, values, hopes, dreams. I sneered at the service's generic quality, lamenting its dependence on hollow, formulaic rituals. I wished the service had been more honest, emotional, and personal.

Like many others before me, I have now learned the truth of the old saying "Be careful what you wish for." Since my friend died, I have attended any number of honest, emotional, personal funerals, most of them so foolish they made my blood run cold. Between the nitwit eulogist, the farewell home video, the flatulent sign-off music, and the inappropriate clothing, funerals have devolved from sacred bonding rituals into commedia dell'arte farces. And it's only going to get worse as more Boomers pass from the scene. . . .

Dreading the Nontraditional Funeral

When I was a child, I dreaded funerals because they were terribly sad. Now I dread them because they're terrible. Having catastrophically mistaken Bill Murray's *Saturday Night Live* skit about a lounge lizard funeral emcee as a viable cultural template, Baby Boomers have transformed the traditional funeral service into a ludicrous stage show: a slapdash mixture of performance art, stand-up comedy, and karaoke. Funerals are no longer somber rituals where we pay our respects to the dead. They are cabaret. They are parties, fun-fests, or what used to be known as happenings. They entail light shows, production numbers, props. They include professionally printed programs complete with sound and lighting credits. They involve the screening of buoyant farewell films comprising inept footage of birthday parties and college graduations that was never meant to be shown in a solemn ceremony. They feature subprofessional singers who seemingly scour the obituaries looking for a chance to cackle "Forever Young" or "Wind Beneath My Wings" over the open casket of a person who obviously had no idea what he was getting into when he died. Most important, they invariably showcase a cavalcade of material-strapped wiseguy eulogists who transform what should be a serious ritual into National Mortuary Open-Mike Night.

It is no secret that Baby Boomers have a hard time dealing with death. A generation whose primary cultural artifact is the Filofax has enormous difficulty shoehorning death into its schedule: It's inconvenient, time-consuming, and stressful. "We don't have time to die this afternoon; Caitlin has ballet." They never could have handled the onerous demands of the Black Death: "So much bubonic plague, so little time." But one also senses a fundamental resentment of the arbitrariness of the universe; if we can get our lives running on schedule, why can't our Higher Power?

Upbeat Funerals—A Way to Conquer Death?

It's equally clear that Boomers are terrified by the thought of a premature, violent, or otherwise untidy demise. A glance at some recent films confirms this. Between 1998 and the summer of 2000, no fewer than six major ghost movies were released by Hollywood. In each of them, a human being had met with an unexpected and, in some cases, gruesome death, and was now seeking vindication, justice, or revenge. In *The Sixth Sense*, Bruce Willis plays a dead psychiatrist who cannot report to The Afterlife for reassignment until he has atoned for a disastrous patient diagnosis that in fact led to his own demise. In *Stir of Echoes*, a raped and strangled teen refuses to evacuate the house where she was murdered until her killers have been brought to justice. In *What Lies Beneath*, it's a murdered coed seeking revenge; in *The Haunting*, it's a bunch of murdered children desperate for vindication; in *Sleepy Hollow*, it's a headless ghost seeking his head. In each case, the dead person refuses to go to his eternal reward until things have reached a satisfactory conclusion back here on planet Earth, because any other denouement would suggest that life is meaningless and that death is capricious, haphazard, and stupid. The subliminal message of these motion pictures is always the same: Just because you're dead doesn't mean you can't get your life organized.

One would have thought that the [Adolf Hitler's] Final Solution, the rape of Nanking, the Mongol invasions, the fall of the Roman Empire, and just about all of human history would have given Baby Boomers a hint that death can be not only a bit messy, but entirely without rhyme or reason. But no, Baby Boomers have decided otherwise: The universe may seem a smidgen incoherent on first glance, but if you roll up your sleeves and attack the problem energetically you can vastly simplify your life. Or death. And one way to accomplish this is through memorable, upbeat funerals.

It must be recalled that ever since the bloodbath known as the Sixties, Baby Boomers have lived in constant fear of anything that threatens to be a downer, a bad scene, or what is technically known as "a drag." They don't like somber funeral services with dim lights and organ music because such grim rituals create the sense that . . . well . . . did somebody just die in here or what? The assumption being that the dead party wouldn't want to do anything to depress his friends. So hey, everybody, let's keep it light. Just have fun with it. Put some more scented oil on the stiff. He ain't dead; he's just mellow.

The Compassionate Death Industry

Unsurprisingly, the search for a death that everyone else can live with has already turned into an industry in some parts of America. "Home deathing" is no longer a novelty; innumerable classes on improving the overall quality of the death experience have sprung up. In San Francisco, people pay $150 for a two-day workshop at the Zen Hospice to learn how to be a compassionate "death companion." The Hospice even has plans to launch a program that will "certify" professional death companions, known as "midwives for death" or "mentors through dying," a role previously handled by the Mafia. As one alternative funeral industry bigwig told the *Wall Street Journal*, their clients "want to personalize and take control of the death experience."

To personalize and take control of the death experience— much as they had earlier personalized and taken control of the urban caffeine experience—Baby Boomers have had to perform some massive retooling of human history. Specifically, they had to throw the Past overboard. Although Boomers are aware that something loosely identified as the Past exists, they have devoted most of their adult lives to pretending that it does not. Contrary to Billy Joel's predictably inaccurate assertion that "we didn't start the fire," Baby Boomers fervently believe that they did, in fact, start the fire, that the world was an incoherent mess before they got here. The Past is nothing more than a series of incomprehensible mistakes, inhabited by people of dubious taste and questionable judgment who do not measure up as human beings when compared to such remarkable people as, say, us.

The way Baby Boomers see it, George Washington and Thomas Jefferson were incorrigible racists whose incidental contributions to the birth of this great nation are completely overshadowed by the mighty deeds of a Martin Luther King or even a Richard Gere. Shakespeare was an anti-Semite, Hemingway a homophobe, Emily Dickinson a wacko, and Mark Twain used the "N-word." None of them are in the same class as Susan Sarandon. Via determinations such as this, Baby Boomers are incessantly heaping derision on the Past in order to justify their fatuous innovations in the Present. And the Past cannot fight back.

Previous generations—say, every single generation dating back to 10,000 B.C.—recognized that history was a fungible resource. They believed that you could learn important things from your forebears: Refrain from sticking your hands in a roaring fire, never let small children play on Mount Vesuvius, think twice before declaring war on the Roman Empire. Then Baby Boomers came along. Adopting a sort of pop Maoism they decided that society must be in a state of permanent upheaval, that its most venerable codes must be repeatedly tested, its traditions reevaluated, its rituals discarded, transmogrified, or reinvented. Nowhere is the fallout from this mind-set more apparent than in the treatment of tragedy.

Uncomfortable with Grief

Start with the lingo. On Saturday, July 8, 2000, newspapers all over America carried reports of the death of Cory Erving, the eighteen-year-old son of basketball immortal Julius Erving. Cory, who had been missing for several weeks, had finally been found dead in a pond not far from the Erving house. Upon receiving this horrible news, Julius Erving is-

sued the following statement: "We are thankful to the Semi-
nole County Sheriff's Office for bringing Cory back to us.
We now have resolution. Getting closure was very important to the family in coping with the loss." He added: "We
have learned a lot from this tragedy, and we will be a
stronger family as a result. The Erving family will go forward from here. We have no other choice."

Avoiding Death: An American Tradition

Although Americans live longer, healthier lives than their
ancestors did—or perhaps because of this—they seem to be
less easy with the prospect of their own mortality. As Evelyn
Waugh observed in *The Loved One*, his bitingly satirical novel
on contemporary funerary practices, we sometimes go to
bizarre and comical lengths to avoid thinking about the one
irreducibly predictable fact of human existence: one day we
shall die. . . .

In short, we seek to banish the terror of death by the simple
device of not dealing with it until we absolutely have to; and
when we are forced to do so, we try to insulate ourselves
from its true significance. In the meantime, the fewer reminders we have of its presence, the better.

Michael M. Uhlmann, *World & I*, July 1998.

With all due respect to Erving, this vacuous statement is
quintessential Boomer blather. Our parents and their parents and everyone's parents were brought up to believe that
when a child dies, the whole universe screams. But Baby
Boomers are so uncomfortable with the language of grief
that they have invented an official funereal twaddle for dealing with precisely such occasions. Tragedy thus becomes another opportunity for character development. A police visit
or lake dredging or autopsy brings us resolution. Instead of
raging against the dying of the light, we are happy for closure. King Lear, we are not.

Over the course of human history, most societies wisely
developed a priestly class whose job it was to preside over
important rituals—many of them unpleasant—and say what
needed to be said in words that would offend the smallest
number of people. Not surprisingly, their most important
work was done at funerals. Though priests and rabbis and

ministers and shamans and even charismatic witch doctors could sometimes rise to the occasion and wax poetic, their basic mission was to hew close to society's most treasured platitudes, providing reassurance to the grieving parties that death was part of life, that life itself had structure and purpose, that death was not a capricious, arbitrary, meaningless, or especially unpleasant event.

Obviously, much of what the clerical class had to say was nonsense, but for the first five thousand years of recorded history this didn't seem to bother anyone. Society at some subconscious level seemed to recognize that even though the high priest could be dull and repetitive and verbose and even vindictive, this was still preferable to letting laymen get into the act. In the course of evolution from shrub-gnawing apes to Sting, societies as diverse as the Mayans, the Maoris, and the Jutes seemed to have agreed on one common point: Funerals are already depressing enough, so let's not make things worse by letting the guy who thinks he's [comedian] Gallagher speak at the service.

The Tag-Team Eulogy

Then along came the Baby Boomers. Convinced of their eloquence, unbending in their belief that they had something to say that nobody else had ever thought of before, Boomers decided that religious figures needed to be purged from the funeral ceremony, or at least marginalized. The result is one of the worst innovations in the history of remorse: the tag-team eulogy. This is the funeral ceremony where as many as two dozen friends of the deceased get up in the pulpit and share their thoughts about the person being buried. Baby Boomers seem incapable of understanding that people attending funerals generally share the same emotions, making it unnecessary for twelve different people to say how much they are going to miss the creature in the casket or urn. But no, everyone has to get up and thank the dead person for "being there."

One funeral I attended featured nine different eulogist headliners. Most of them did a fairly good job under the circumstances; they were funny, tender, warm, affectionate. But one aspiring Mark Antony had to opt for Door Number

Three. He chose to recount a conversation he'd had with his now-departed friend shortly before he died. The deceased had recently recovered from a long illness and was now on the mend. He had a new job that he genuinely enjoyed. He was working on a raftload of exciting projects that had recently been moved off the back burner. He honestly believed that he had turned the corner and was very excited about what life held in store for him. Then he died. The eulogist concluded this reverie with the words: "It reminds me of that old saying: If you want to make God laugh, tell him about your plans."

This philosophical bon mot constitutes what used to be known as a "bummer" or a "bring down." The speaker has already established his personal bona fides, demonstrating beyond a shadow of a doubt that he has standing to speak about the deceased. He has beguiled the mourners with his witty repartee and a tasteful assortment of colorful anecdotes. He has opened his heart; he has shared. Now all he needs to do is to get off the stage. But no, he has to push the envelope. First, despite the fact that this is a rigorously nonsectarian service, he has to get in a little dig at the Creator. This always gets things off to a good start. Then, whether he is aware of it or not, he goes out of his way to show disrespect for the person he has come to eulogize. "What a jerk you were for thinking you were finally getting your act together! Don't you know that this is an indifferent universe, where life is meaningless and death even more so? Don't you know how things work on this planet? Jesus Christ Almighty, what is it with you?"

Maybe it's time for funeral directors to start vetting these speeches.

Conflicting Theologies

Another unfortunate Baby Boomer contribution to the mortuary arts is the theologically eclectic funeral service. It has long been my belief that people should be buried in the rites of the religion least likely to embarrass them. But because Baby Boomers are all over the lot philosophy-wise, I have often had to attend services where the various liturgies not only war with each other but sometimes cancel one another out. Because we Baby Boomers believe in nothing, we end up acting like we believe in everything. Funeral services thus become a religious smorgasbord. This is not good.

Personally speaking, once I've heard the sparse Quaker prayer and the lugubrious Kaddish reading and a couple of unpublished poems by some tribal elder from Manitoba, I don't have the energy left to gut out the Seventh Sutra of the Sun. Often I come away from these services more confused and saddened than when I went in. First, I'm told that my friend is just another form of energy. Then I find that he's up there looking down on us. No, that's not right, he's gone to a far, far better place. No, his spirit is breathing in the daffodils just outside the window. No, he's stone dead, so get used to it. One time I was so distraught upon returning from a spectacularly multicultural funeral that I went into my closet, yanked out a baseball bat, and handed it to my fourteen-year-old son.

"Gord, I want you to make me a promise," I said. "I want you to promise me that when I die, if anyone gets up at my funeral and mentions the *I Ching*, the *Bhagavad-Gita*, or the *Tibetan Book of the Dead*, or if anyone even so much as suggests that I am not dead but have just transmuted myself into another form of energy, or if anyone implies that I was just chomping at the bit to meet my Maker, that I felt a tremor of bliss, that in those last weeks and months I almost seemed to be letting go, then please take this baseball bat and break their legs. And if anyone dares to mention the word 'sutra' at my funeral you have my permission to kill them."

"Cool," was my son's reply.

In my perhaps outmoded view, for a funeral to truly work two things are necessary. First off, a modicum of respect must be shown. Here I am talking about contemporary funeral attire. Last year, I attended a service where two middle-aged men were wearing New York Giants windbreakers. No matter who is being buried, this is unacceptable mourning garb. For one, it's tasteless and shows a lack of breeding. Two, the Giants finished 6–10 that season and didn't even make the playoffs. What kind of message does that send to the kids? Or to the dead person? The lesson to be learned is simple: If you don't care enough about the dearly departed to put on a suit and a tie, then stay home. This is doubly true for Cleveland Browns fans.

Second, it is necessary for at least one person to admit that he is actually going to miss the dead person. I am not suggesting that we need to go overboard, with the rending of clothing and the tearing of hair and the gnashing of teeth. But for a dead person to get the send-off he deserves, at least one person actually has to break down and cry. If it is not possible for the mother, children, or significant other to do this, I suggest that survivors start hiring official mourners to provide an aura of grief at funerals. I am sure they can be found in Northern California. One of my friends has even suggested holding two funerals for every person that dies: one for the weepy types, the other for the mourners on Prozac. Of course, there are always those who make a point of never attending funeral services, because, as they so cleverly put it, "I don't do grief." For them, e-funerals should do very well indeed.

*"There is wide acknowledgment that
bereavement can . . . lead to . . . depression
and anxiety. Thus . . . professional
intervention may be especially important."*

Medical Treatment May Reduce the Pain of Grief

Katherine Shear

Katherine Shear is a professor of psychiatry at the University of Pittsburgh School of Medicine and director of the school's Panic, Anxiety, and Traumatic Grief Program. In the following viewpoint, she maintains that grief is similar to a physical illness and should be treated by mental health professionals in some cases. According to Shear, people coping with the sudden, violent death of a loved one are particularly vulnerable to depression and may require antidepressant medication and/or psychotherapy. Early medical intervention will help restore the bereaved's hopefulness for the future and social function, in the author's opinion.

As you read, consider the following questions:

1. What "commonalities" characterize the grieving process, according to Shear?
2. In the author's opinion, how is grief analogous to a physical injury?
3. What steps should mental health professionals take to help individuals suffering from the sudden or violent loss of a loved one, as listed by the author?

Excerpted from "Managing Grief After Disaster," by Katherine Shear, www.ncptsd.org.

Grief is the process by which we adjust to the loss of a close relationship and so is an inevitable companion to love and attachment. The lives of those we love are interwoven with our own in thousands of small and large ways. One's immediate family, in particular, contribute to a sense of comfort, security and happiness and serve as reinforcers of behavior. Endocrine function can become entrained to cues from another person. If so, losing that person requires a period of physiological adjustment. In all cases, loss of a loved one engenders feelings of loneliness, sadness and vulnerability. The death of someone close also makes one's own death imaginable, thus evoking fear of dying. Acute separation distress and confrontation with mortality, are always present, to a greater or lesser degree, in the aftermath of the death of someone close. Sometimes, there is also guilt about being alive when the other person has died, or about failure to save the person who died or to make their life or their dying easier.

The Experience of Grief

While grief is not the same for every person, there are certain commonalities. During the initial phase, the bereaved person is preoccupied with the deceased, with feelings of yearning, longing and searching for him or her. While grieving, most people withdraw from the world and turn inward, often reviewing the course of the relationship including positive and negative thoughts and feelings, as well as the meaning the relationship had in their lives. Grief entails a host of painful emotions that can sometimes be very strong and persistent. Strong feelings of sadness and loneliness almost always occur following the death of a close friend or family member. Fear and anxiety are also common, especially in confronting death. Difficult feelings of resentment, anger, and guilt can occur. Experiencing any or all of these emotions following the loss of a friend or family member is perfectly normal.

As the transition to life without a friend or family member progresses, the intensity of grief subsides. The bereaved person accepts the death and begins to take some comfort in positive memories, establishing a permanent sense of connection to the person who died. It becomes possible to re-engage in activities and relationships, keeping memories and a sense of closeness to the deceased. The period over which this adjustment occurs is variable, depending on circumstances of the death, characteristics of the bereaved, and the nature of the relationship. In some circumstances, intense grief persists for many months or even years. Intrusive images and disturbing ideas inhibit the healing process, and there is a sense that the death is unacceptable and unfair. For some who have difficulty coping with the death, grief sometimes seems to be all there is left of the relationship. For others, decreasing intensity of grief feels like a betrayal of the person who died. Still others have persistent feelings of guilt. When a death is sudden, violent and untimely, difficulties are more likely to occur. The condition in which unmanageably intense and/or persistent grief symptoms occur is called Traumatic Grief. Symptoms of Traumatic Grief are listed in Table 1. Work is underway to establish diagnostic criteria and develop treatments for this condition. Traumatic Grief may predispose to other psychiatric, medical and behavioral problems that can complicate bereavement. These are generally treatable conditions and need to

Table 1: Symptoms of Traumatic Grief	
Preoccupation with the deceased	Pain in the same area as the deceased
Memories are upsetting	Avoid reminders of the death
Death is unacceptable	Feeling life is empty
Longing for the person	Hear the voice of the person who died
Drawn to places and things associated with the deceased	See the person who died
Anger about the death	Feel it is unfair to live when this person died
Disbelief about the death	Bitter about the death
Feeling stunned or dazed	Envious of others
Difficulty trusting others	Lonely most of the time
Difficulty caring about others	

be recognized by professionals, as well as bereaved individuals themselves.

Complications of Bereavement

Bereavement is a risk factor for a range of mental and physical health problems. Among these are the following:

Prolonged or "Traumatic" Grief
- Onset or recurrence of Major Depression
- Onset or recurrence of Panic Disorder or other Anxiety Disorders
- Possible increased vulnerability to post-traumatic stress disorder (PTSD)
- Alcohol and other Substance use
- Smoking, poor nutrition, low levels of exercise
- Suicidal ideation
- Onset or worsening of health problems, especially cardiovascular and immunologic dysfunction

Traumatic Grief

Disruption in mental functioning from grief is inevitable following death of a loved one. While it should be stressed that grief itself is a normal process of adapting emotionally and cognitively to the loss or absence of a loved one, sometimes the intensity of a person's grief may be overwhelming or last longer than it should. This may occur for a variety of reasons. The relationship might be very close or complicated; the circumstances of the death may be sudden or traumatic as in accident, disaster or illness; or the grieving person may not have a history of good coping skills or social support that would help the grieving process. At times like these, it may be helpful to seek professional help or counseling in order to resolve the grief.

When grief goes on longer than it should or is overwhelming, a diagnosis of traumatic grief might be appropriate. [It] may be helpful to draw an analogy to a physical illness. An illness is not a characteristic of a person, it is a state a person is in at a given time. Many illnesses are very treatable. Another analogy is to an acute injury. People are more or less vulnerable to disability from injury, but some types of injury are so severe that they always cause impairment. Using such analogy, it is possible to see that following circumstances of an accident or disaster, or the sudden death of a very close person, it is entirely normal to experience Traumatic Grief, just as it is quite normal to develop tuberculosis upon exposure to a virulent organism, and normal to be unable to walk on a broken leg. It is also clear that it is a good idea to diagnose and treat these conditions. No one would tell a person with pneumonia to pull "yourself together" or "get on with it" or expect a person with a deep cut or a broken bone to heal themselves. Although labels can be hurtful if misused, they can also be helpful. An ill person needs to have a "sick role" and to receive treatment. An ill person benefits from support and assistance from family and friends, as well as treatment by a trained professional. . . .

Treatment of Bereaved Individuals

Grief support groups and grief counseling is widespread and undoubtedly highly variable. Little information is available related to its outcome. There is specific controversy regarding the importance of confronting the death (also called "grief work") in the early phase of grief. In one study investigators developed a measure to assess the extent to which individuals confronted or avoided their loss and used scores on this instrument to predict outcome at later times. They found that low scores for widows did not influence outcome, but low scores for widowers predicted poorer outcome. There is some evidence that the occurrence of symptoms of major depression in the first month following the death predicts a worse course later, especially for suicidally bereaved.

It goes without saying that the loss of a close relationship permanently affects the bereaved person. It is not reasonable to think that one would "recover" from such a loss, nor to think one could "resolve" the loss. Such a loss is permanent and has permanent effects on the bereaved. Still, it is possible and probably important that the bereaved person eventually feel interested and able to engage in life and to have comforting memories of the deceased. Weiss (1993) provides a list of reasonable expectations, including 1) ability to give energy to everyday life, 2) psychological comfort, or freedom from pain and distress, 3) ability to experience satisfaction and gratification in life, 4) hopefulness for the future, and 5) ability to function adequately in a range of social roles. How then can a professional assist in achieving these goals?

Early Intervention

There is little data on the effectiveness of early intervention for grief, but it is clear that early intervention is a good idea following a disaster, provided it is administered by a skilled, empathic clinician. Though data suggests that even after sudden, violent death, most people eventually grieve successfully, this can take a long time. Many people consider grief to be a personal experience, similar to love. Most people do not turn to mental health professionals to tell them how to love, nor do they look for help with grief. However, when a loss is sudden and violent, the intensity of emotions can be frightening and the need for support and outside intervention greater. In response, the professional needs to use a skilled, supportive intervention. Useful components of such intervention include

- Providing information about grief, its symptoms, course and complications
- Evaluating the nature of the individual's distress
- Helping to identify and problem solve practical matters
- Providing strategies for management of intense affect
- Assist the person to think about the death in a way that leads to emotional resolution

Affect-evoking interventions must be used with care and expert skill, balanced with containing and soothing strategies. During the early phase a brief intervention providing information and strategies for thinking about the death may be very useful; it is best if the professional provides some follow-up and remains available for consultation and support, should this be needed.

Prigerson and Jacobs provide a useful list of "do's" and "don'ts" for physicians following a patient's death. These can also be useful to consider. They suggest

- Direct expression of sympathy
- Acknowledgement that the clinician does not know what the bereaved person is "going through"

- Talking about the deceased, including saying his or her name
- Eliciting questions about the circumstances of the death
- Eliciting questions about feelings and about how the death has affected the person

A useful list of cautions about things that are **NOT HELPFUL** is also provided and includes:

- A casual or passive attitude (e.g. "call me" or asking "how are you")
- Statements that the death is in any way for the best, or acceptable (e.g. "He/she is in a better place" or "it's God's will")
- Assumption that the bereaved is strong and will/should get through this
- Any kind of avoidance of discussion of the death or the person who died

Even given its private nature, variable course and usual resolution, there are circumstances in which grief can be intense and prolonged, hindering re-engagement in daily activities. When this occurs, a focused intervention may be needed. There is wide acknowledgment that bereavement can be prolonged and also that it can lead to other mental health problems, especially depression and anxiety. Thus, for a high risk group professional intervention may be especially important.

Treatment Strategies

Treatment should target the symptoms experienced by the patient. It is now very clear that bereaved who experience Major Depression (MDD) respond to antidepressant medication and/or psychotherapy, similarly to those who are not bereaved. A very interesting recent study suggests that treatment of MDD as early as a month after the death, may be extremely helpful and prevent later symptoms. Similarly, for those who meet criteria for PTSD it makes sense to provide treatment similar to other PTSD patients. However, the most common problems of post-bereavement centers around traumatic grief reactions, and unfortunately, few treatments have been developed or tested for symptoms of Traumatic Grief. Studies of early intervention for grief document some reduction in grief symptoms, with support groups showing efficacy equal to that of active psychotherapy. An early study of a behavioral therapy called "guided mourning" also appeared to have beneficial effects though grief outcome was not measured. A specific "Traumatic Grief Treatment (TGT)" is currently undergoing randomized controlled testing. In a pilot study, TGT had a large effect size, even taking into consideration individuals who did not complete the full course of the treatment. Components of this treatment include

- Information about bereavement and grief for bereaved individuals and their families
- Description of the deceased and history of the relationship with the deceased
- Story of the death and its aftermath
- Careful assessment of current grief levels, target grief level and components of grief (i.e. cognitive, behavioral and somatic)
- Review of Personal Goals and how the bereaved person will know when these have been met
- Carefully managed imaginal exposure to the death and related events
- In vivo exposure to situations that are avoided and/or response prevention for situations of preoccupation
- Focus on positive memories of the deceased . . .

It is also important to gain an idea of the social support system of the bereaved person and to support engagement with existing supportive people. At this time there has been no treatment proven effective in early stages of bereavement and some indication that for some people formal grief counselling can cause more harm than good. In this light, caution may be indicated.

Guidelines for early treatment in the acute phase of a traumatic grief would include giving an opportunity for the bereaved person to talk about the nature and circumstances of their loss according to their own readiness (without probing); educating about the course of bereavement and what to expect; assessing for possible troubling symptoms like unusual intensity of grief reactions or intrusive thoughts; encouraging social support and broadening of activities as much as possible without intruding; and encouraging positive memories and connection to the deceased to help supplant traumatic memories.

Pharmacotherapy may also be helpful to individuals suffering from Traumatic Grief. However, little has been done to test pharmacotherapy. It appears that, as for depression and PTSD, there is some beneficial effect of serotonin active medications. Given available information, it seems important that clinicians learn to administer techniques that appear to be efficacious. Training programs are under development in the affected areas.

"Grief is not like an illness, to be fought and cured with medicine or chemotherapy and radiation. . . . Each person's grieving process is unique."

Grief Cannot Be Managed

Stephanie Salter

Stephanie Salter maintains in the following viewpoint that the grieving process following the death of a loved one is unique for each person and does not conform to a predictable "healing" pattern. Instead of covering up grief with medication, the bereaved should be encouraged to openly grieve without being pressured to get over their loss in a limited time frame, in Salter's opinion. The author is a columnist with the *San Francisco Chronicle*.

As you read, consider the following questions:
1. In Salter's opinion, how do Americans typically deal with grief?
2. What is unique about the grief support provided by the Compassionate Friends organization, according to the author?

Not long ago, a friend in New York said that she often feels cut off from the rest of the country because [the terrorist attack of] September 11 is still so much with most New Yorkers.

Few Formal Grieving Rituals

"We've all gotten on with our lives, and if you don't go down to the (World Trade Center) site, there are no visible traces," she said. "But there's still so much grief and sadness hanging in the air."

People outside of New York can't really understand, said my friend.

"You talk with them and, if you didn't lose someone directly in the twin towers, it's like their tone says, 'Hey, shouldn't you be moving on?' They don't get that there's a collective grief. I actually prefer it when people don't even ask how it's going. It's easier."

Our American culture boasts many virtues and several strong suits, but grieving—collectively or individually—isn't one of them.

Unlike older societies, we have few formal grieving rituals in place to guide us. So, we try to tackle grief in our typical American way—as if it's a problem to be solved, an illness to be cured, an unnatural, machine-gumming breakdown that needs to be fixed, ASAP.

Perhaps more phobic about suffering than any society in history, Americans tend to start the clock ticking early in "managing" grief. While solicitous and caring of the newly bereaved, we encourage heartbroken mates and parents to medicate themselves so they can "keep it together" through the funeral.

This ignores the fact that wailing and keening and "losing it" are a pretty accurate rendering of what humans inside feel like when someone we love dies or leaves us. But, in our culture, public wailing and keening are considered bad forms; they are seen as unwelcome reminders of pathology among "healthy" people.

Even the most devastating loss—that of a child by a parent—seems to carry an unwritten statute of limitations on grief, something I learned several years ago when I reported on an international organization called Compassionate Friends.

Founded in England in the late 1960s, the massive support network's chapters provide something that bereaved parents and siblings can't get from the rest of the world: "unconditional love and understanding" (as its informal credo states) with no expiration date.

Get Over It? The Wrong Media Message

[One] message from the media is the belief that people who experience the tragic death of their loved ones need to get through it, accept it, recover, and close. In a February 1999 segment of ABC's *20/20*, the reporter said a couple whose six children were killed because of the actions of an illegally licensed driver had turned "their grief into action." What a magic trick! Now you see grief and—voila—it turns into action. The parents of the children who died, anchor Hugh Downs added, are "God-fearing people and they relied on their faith to get them through the loss of their six children." Of course we never actually hear the grieving parents say the words, "*get us through* the loss of our six children." In fact, in my twenty years of working with bereaved parents I have never heard a parent say, "I've got to get through the death of my child." As the story continued, another word came up: "But their struggle for acceptance would be disturbed by a series of anonymous phone calls. . . ." Few people would dare to ask a bereaved parent, "Have you accepted the death of your child?" Yet the media continue to slip it in.

Robert Baugher, *Columbia Journalism Review*, March/April 2001.

As one member told me, she knew that a Compassionate Friends meeting was the one place she could go and never hear the unintentionally accusing question, "How many years ago did you say your child died?"

The Tidal Wave of Grief

Grief is not like an illness, to be fought and cured with medicine or chemotherapy and radiation. Generalizations can be made about human behavioral tendencies, and time lines can be drawn for predicted "healing," but each person's grieving process is unique.

Some people never "get better." And nobody survives grief unchanged.

As Stephanie Ericsson wrote in [the 1993 book] *Companion Through the Darkness*, grief is "a tidal wave that overtakes you, smashes down upon you with unimaginable force, sweeps you up into its darkness, where you tumble and crash against unidentifiable surfaces only to be thrown out on an unknown beach, bruised, reshaped."

Or, as a man who lost his 7-year-old son once confided, "I'd always thought of myself as a happy man, but that's gone now. We have moments of happiness, some of them long and filled with laughter, but the sense of what is lost is never far away."

In her book, Stephanie Ericsson also warned:

"Grief makes what others think of you moot. It shears away the masks of normal life and forces brutal honesty out of your mouth before propriety can stop you. It shoves away friends and scares away so-called friends and rewrites your address book for you."

Periodical Bibliography

The following articles have been selected to supplement the diverse views presented in this chapter.

Brian Appleyard	"How Cold Our Hearts Have Grown," *New Statesman*, January 14, 2002.
Beth Baker	"Mourning in America," *Common Boundary*, May/June 1999.
Nate Barker	"Facing Death," *Christian Social Action*, January/February 2001.
B. Bower	"Good Grief: Bereaved Adjust Well Without Airing Emotion," *Science News*, March 2, 2002.
John A. Cutter	"Waiting to Die," *San Diego Union-Tribune*, May 1, 1998.
Julia Duin	"Avoiding Death: Americans Tend to Put Lives Ahead of the Inevitable," *Washington Times*, February 13, 2002.
Steve Emmons	"Mourning: Baby Boomers Shop Around, Buy Direct, Cremate More—and Even Engage in Some Do-It-Yourself," *Los Angeles Times*, December 7, 1998.
Erica Goode	"Experts Offer Fresh Insights into the Mind of the Grieving Child," *New York Times*, March 28, 2000.
Ellen Goodman	"Coming Soon: The One-Minute Mourner," *Los Angeles Times*, January 6, 1998.
Susan Grelock	"Moving Through Grief," *Natural Health*, March 2000.
Ellen A. Grollman	"Explaining Death to Children," *Moment*, October 1999.
Dan Kennedy	"Coping with Loss: Teachings of a Master," *World*, July/August 2000.
Richard Lichtman	"Dying in America," *Tikkun*, July/August 2001.
Tim Matson	"The Last Thing You Want to Do," *Mother Earth News*, August/September 2001.
Lisa Miller	"Boomers Begin to Look Beyond the Good Life to the 'Good Death,'" *Wall Street Journal*, February 25, 2000.
Richard John Neuhaus	"Born Toward Dying," *First Things*, February 2000.
Sara Rimer	"Looking at Death with Old Age Near," *New York Times*, September 30, 1999.

Should Effort to Expand the Human Life Span Be Pursued?

Chapter Preface

In the early sixteenth century, Spanish explorer Juan Ponce de Leon led an expedition from the island of Borinquen, later renamed Puerto Rico, in search of a magical spring known as "the fountain of youth." According to legend, a drink from the spring's waters would restore youth and vigor. Ponce de Leon never found the fountain of youth, but he did discover what he believed to be an island, which he named La Florida. In actuality, this "island" turned out to be the west coast of the Florida peninsula, a region of the country now associated more with elderly retirees than youthful vigor.

Ponce de Leon's expedition may have failed, but thousands of Americans have continued the search for the elusive fountain of youth. Refusing to accept death as a natural and inevitable fact of life, proponents of life-extension techniques are convinced that science may one day uncover the secrets to the aging process. This growing movement of "extropians" and "transhumanists" strives to challenge conventional thinking about human aging through the use of new technologies. They hope to postpone death by proactively seeking out the right combination of pills, elixirs, genetic engineering, and even a post-mortem preservation technique known as "cryonics," to make their dream a reality. Explains Alex Heard, an editor with the *New York Times Magazine*, "[A] small but fervent subculture of Americans . . . are convinced that science will deliver superlongevity within the next few decades, and [they are] determined to hang on for it. . . . 'Life extension' [is] a blanket term for a bulky pile of personal-health regimens and futuristic enthusiasms about technology's potential."

As the president of the Extropy Institute Max More explains, the life-extension movement is based on a steadfast optimism that by defeating death, humans can add new meaning and value to their existence. Says More, "Aging and death victimizes all humans. . . . The infuriating truth is that, just as we begin to accumulate a modicum of wisdom and skill, aging sneaks in to sap our energies. . . . Thus, to extropians and other transhumanists, the technological conquest of aging and death stands out as the most urgent, vital, worthy quest of time." More maintains that the desire for immortality should be regarded as part of the natural human drive to "transform ourselves and our environment." He argues that fulfilling the natural drive for transcendence will allow human life and intelligence to flourish.

The life-extension movement, however, is not without its critics; many observers question whether defeating death is a desirable goal. Richard L. Landau and James M. Gustafson, professors of medicine and divinity, respectively, at the University of Chicago, argue that death should not be regarded as an enemy. They maintain that "an intense preoccupation with the preservation of physical life . . . seems to be based on an assumption that death is unnatural, or that its delay, . . . through medical and technical means is always a triumph of human achievement over the limitations of nature." According to their view, nature never intended for humans to live a prolonged, "grotesque, fragmented, or inordinately expensive existence."

With ever advancing technology, people will most likely be living longer and longer lives, but the effects of postponing death remain undetermined. For example, expanded human life spans may contribute to a host of societal problems, such as overpopulation and questions of who gets access to youth-maintaining treatments. In the following chapter, whether or not human life should be extended is debated.

| "We face a new millennium in which . . .
aging will become first preventable and
then reversible."

Immortality Is an Achievable and Worthy Goal

Frank R. Zindler

In the following viewpoint, Frank R. Zindler contends that scientific advances will greatly extend the human life span and may one day make immortality feasible. According to Zindler, researchers have made significant progress in understanding how genes can be turned on and off to disrupt the aging process. In addition, scientists have come closer to discovering biological agents, such as the molecule aminoguanidine, that can actually reverse aging. The author maintains that an extended life span is within the reach of those persons who seek out new anti-aging technologies. Zindler is a former professor of biology and a member of the American Association for the Advancement of Science.

As you read, consider the following questions:

1. What word did the author coin to describe self-destruct genes?
2. According to Zindler, how long could a "ferox human" expect to live?
3. What is the "Holy Grail" of aging research that scientists are beginning to uncover, in the author's opinion?

Excerpted from "The Prospects for Physical Immortality," by Frank R. Zindler, *American Atheist*, Winter 1998–1999. Copyright © 1998 by American Atheist Press. Reprinted with permission.

M ust we all die? This is a question which humankind in all ages have asked. In the Western world, the answer to this question has almost invariably been "yes." What is, after all, more obvious than our mortality? To be sure, our mythologies are replete with characters such as Adam and Methuselah, who were imagined to have succeeded in eluding The Reaper for a number of centuries. But, significantly, even they at last cashed in their chips.

Our religions, for the most part, have given up hope for physical immortality altogether and have invented "spiritual" immortality as a rather anemic substitute for which to hope. Since eternity with neither bodies nor brains is hard to market, some religions have added the doctrine of bodily resurrection. But there is something profoundly immaterial about the bodies we will be issued when we're mustered up beside the plastic petunias in Forest Lawn. Certainly our new bodies will not be equipped for fornication, and it is unthinkable that a resurrected Christian will recommence to urinate and defecate! Sneezing and sweating, too, seem unseemly passtimes for new-issue bodies. By the time one subtracts all the activities the resurrected "bodies" are not likely to perform, the bodies seem hardly to be bodies at all! . . .

Admitting the biological necessity for death in the past, is death still necessary? Is death still desirable? (Only biologists and manic-depressives ask such questions!) Is death still inevitable, now that we have become a form of life conscious of itself—aware of its origins and using the insights of science to chart its future course?

It Ain't Necessarily So

I believe the answers to all these questions is an emphatic "*No!*" We no longer need to die. Mortality is not an *a priori* necessity. Biology should enable us to become essentially immortal. As we approach the year 2,000, we have already made astonishing break-throughs in the understanding of aging. We face a new millennium in which—as I shall try to show—aging will become first preventable and then reversible. . . .

In trying to justify my hope that essential immortality should be achievable very soon, I must declare the subject of "accidental" death to be beyond the scope of my discussion.

A person run over by a steamroller in the year 2,020 will be just as dead as the one run over in 1998. I shall, therefore, limit my discussion to the kind of death conceived to be the terminus of old age.

"*Senectus ipse morbus est*" ("Old age is itself a sickness") said the Roman poet Terence, who flourished in the second century B.C. "Old age is itself a sickness," echo the majority of modern biologists. No longer believing that sickness comes either from god or the devil, biologists now view aging and death as just another disease in need of cure—just like small-pox, cholera, or cancer.

Self-Destruct Genes

While the sickness model of aging and death may prove unable to explain everything, it is a good place to begin. In order to cure any disease, it is usually necessary to identify the causative agent and discern the nature of the damage which must be repaired. To fight effectively, one must first know the enemy. To cure aging, we must first seek out its causes.

Fortunately, we do not have to look very far in order to get lots of ideas about the causes of aging. There are some things which practically leap up to capture our attention.

Consider salmon, for instance.

Salmon are hatched in freshwater streams, develop, and then descend to the sea to grow to sexual maturity. As much as five years after their birth, the nubile fish reascend the rivers which gave them life to consummate their nuptials. At this time a most remarkable transformation occurs. The formerly sleek, silvery-blue fish become a dull, reddish brown. The males in particular become ugly and misshapen. As the fish spawn, they grow suddenly old. Most die within a few days after the fertilization of the eggs. Rare indeed is the salmon that survives to spawn again. It is as though the fish had happened into a never-sought-for Fountain of Senility.

Similar to the case of the salmon, though even more dramatic, is the case of the mayflies. These insects are classified in an order named *Ephemerida*, in recognition of their ephemeral existence. All but one or two days of their entire lives are spent as aquatic larvae. At last they emerge from the water, try out their new-found wings, perpetuate their race—and perish. Within hours, their temporary terrestrial tenure is at an end.

And then there are carrots.

Carrots, as everyone knows, are *biennial* plants. That is, they live exactly two years, flower, go to seed, and die. They die not at the end of one year, nor at the end of three. Almost always, they self-destruct at the end of two years. A similar, but more impressive phenomenon, is seen in the so-called "seventeen-year locust"—actually a cicada—which lives for sixteen years as a larva, emerges as an adult in its seventeenth year, mates, and seeks out a recycling service for its carbon atoms.

Is there any relationship between salmon, mayflies, cicadas, and carrots? I think so. The precision with which their aging and death occur makes one suspect that there is some sort of genetic predestination at work. It is as though evolution has equipped these species with self-destruct genes whose function is to get older generations out of the way in order to avoid competition with their descendants.

Coin a Word

Back in the early 1980s, when I first started writing on this subject, no technical word for such self-destruct genes existed, and so I coined one. I termed them *opsephoneal* genes (from the Greek, *opse*, meaning "late" and *phoneus*, meaning "murderer"). Alas, the term has not caught on, even though (as we shall see) such genes have at least something to do with aging in all animal species.

Are opsephoneal genes at work in human aging?

While humans are neither annual nor biennial, they are—if I may be permitted the barbarism—proverbially three-score-and-tennial. While improved care and nutrition have steadily increased man's life *expectancy*, they have not significantly increased his life *span*. That is still nearly fixed at about seventy years, although some recent authors feel the human life-span really to be about 110 years. (The world record is held by a French lady who died recently at the age of 122.) This reinforces the suspicion that opsephoneal genes are at work.

The suspicion is further strengthened by the bizarre disease known as Werner's progeria—premature old age. By the age of eight, a child may be biologically eighty. It seems as though something has happened to activate prematurely a normally dormant opsephoneal gene. It seems not irrational to suppose, therefore, that if something can turn *on* such a gene prematurely, we should be able to find a way to turn *off*—or at least delay such a gene as well.

Many people, when discussing the genetic aspect of aging with me, express the hope that aging will *not* prove to be genetically predestined. They shrink from the notion as if it were a sort of biological Calvinism. "What hope can we have if our very genes are against us?" they ask.

Actually, if suicide genes were the whole story, we would be in great luck. For we already know a great deal about what turns genes on and off. Hormones, for instance, are busy at this moment turning on and off various of the reader's genes as he reads these words. Other genes are turned on or off as a result of the buildup of various, simple chemicals in the cell. Still other genes may be inhibited by large protein molecules located at strategic positions in the nucleus of the cell.

Turn It Off

Most exciting of all, genetic engineers have learned to read and write in genetic code. It is now a daily occurrence for human genes (made of DNA) to be combined with particular synthetic or natural sequences of DNA which will guarantee expression (turning on) of the gene in a new host cell, say, a bacterium. That which genetic engineers turn on, can be turned off as well. In any event, if aging and death were due to the action of suicide genes alone, the cure for old age would be conceptually no more complicated than finding the legendary Fountain of Youth. All we would need to do would be to find a drug or some other form of "magic bullet" which was specific for the gene in question and was able either to repress it or permanently disarm it. . . .

Discovery of Genes Controlling Aging

The existence of "suicide genes" has been proven beyond any room for doubt—at least at the cellular level. It has been known for many years that embryonic development is accompanied by the "programmed death" of large numbers of cells. Called *apoptosis* in the technical language of cell biology, scheduled death of particular cells allows for the movements and migrations of other cells as they seek out the positions they will occupy in the mature body. It has been discovered also that the body has an apoptotic defense system for fighting viral infections and stopping cancer before it can get out of control. In the case of cancer defense, apoptosis causes the self-destruction of cells before they can start proliferating. Cancers develop when something interferes with the signalling system that "decides" when apoptosis-triggering genes need to be activated. An enormous amount of medical research is now being carried out to discover drugs that can induce apoptosis where needed, drugs that can turn on suicide genes. Once this is all sorted out, we should also be able to deal with the reverse problem: turning *off* suicide genes being activated in tissues that we don't want to lose, *e.g.*, healthy brain tissue.

Concerning the discovery of genes associated with the aging process in general, the last two years [1997–1998] have produced so many discoveries in so many different areas that it is hard to know how to deal with it all. Earlier I noted the curious phenomenon of sudden aging in salmon. It has recently been discovered that in brown trout (a close relative of the salmon) fish possessing a particular form of a gene for the enzyme lactic dehydrogenase (*Ldh*-5) develop a giant, "ferox" body form—and live about five times longer than the smaller trout which have a "normal" form of the gene. If this could be extrapolated to humans, we would expect a "ferox human" to live 350 years!

In the tiny roundworm *Caenorhabditis elegans*, a bunch of genes have been discovered which can greatly affect the life expectancy of the humble creature. Mutations in these genes have been produced that can greatly increase longevity by—you guessed it!—increasing resistance to free radicals [reactive particles produced by oxygen that attack cells], ultraviolet light, and other stressors. The first of these, *age*-1, has been identified with the enzyme phosphatidylinositol 3-kinase and produces a life expectancy about double that of worms possessing the normal form of the gene. Another mutation, *daf*-2, affects a gene resembling that for the insulin receptor and may provide an explanation for the increase in longevity associated with food restriction in many animal species. A number of so-called "clock mutations" have also been discovered in this worm that can increase life expectancy. The first of these, *clk*-1, encodes a protein that indirectly regulates the transcription of genes controlling energy metabolism. Combinations of these mutations, such as *daf*-2, with *clk*-1, increase longevity five-fold! Would human analogs of these mutations give us life expectancies of 350 years? Gene switching that causes these worms to go into a sort of slow-motion *dauer* state resembling hibernation can increase longevity eight-fold—the equivalent of 560 years in humans!

A rather startling discovery was made in June of 1998 when it was learned that transplanting the *human* gene *SOD*1 into the nerve cells of fruitflies could increase lifespans as much as 40 percent. Significantly, the enzyme encoded by this gene is superoxide dismutase, which has the job of chemically disarming superoxide, a particularly dangerous free-radical form of oxygen. . . .

The importance of enzymes able to disarm free radicals was underscored late in August of 1998 when Naoaki Ishii of Tokai University Medical School in Japan discovered a mutation in a *C. elegans* gene called *mev*-1 which causes worms to die sooner when exposed to excess oxygen. The mutation allows excessive production and build up of free radicals in mitochondria, the powerhouses of cells.

Mortal and Immortal Cell Lines

Moving up to mammals, in November of 1997, Tokyo researcher Makoto Kuro-o and colleagues reported the discovery of a mouse gene they called *klotho*, named after Klotho, one of the Fates of Greek mythology. A defect in this gene produces a syndrome resembling human aging, including a short lifespan, infertility, arteriosclerosis, skin degeneration, osteoporosis, and emphysema.

The genetic basis of Werner's progeria, mentioned earlier, has been found to involve a gene resembling those encoding enzymes known as DNA helicases. Mutations leading to loss of function of this gene impair DNA replication or repair—producing the premature aging phenomena associated with this fortunately rare disease. Significantly, this gene mutation is also associated with a rapid decrease in the length of *telomeres*—long DNA structures at the ends of chromosomes that seem to be the functional equivalents of the caps placed at the ends of shoelaces to prevent fraying and unraveling.

Life Expectancy, 1900–2050

(life expectancy at birth by sex in U.S., 1900–1975, and middle-series projection, 2000–2050)

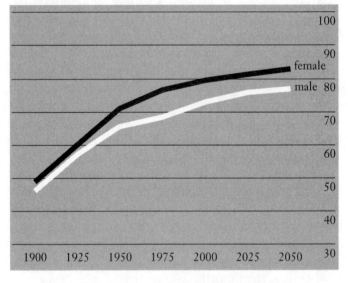

Since 1900, life expectancy at birth has increased by almost 30 years. By 2050, it could increase another 5 years.

Brad Edmondson, *American Demographics*, April 1997.

It has long been known that the telomeres are associated with the ability of cells to reproduce in tissue-culture situations. Most cells, when placed in culture, are able to divide just so many times. After a certain number of generations, the cells "senesce," decline, and die. Other cells—cancer cells, for example—seem to be able to reproduce forever in culture. Somehow, the changes that converted normal cells into cancer cells "immortalized" them. It is now fairly well established that the difference between mortal and immortal cell lines involves changes in telomere maintenance. Each time that an ordinary cell divides, its telomeres become a bit shorter. Finally, the telomere is too short to protect the chromosome to which it is attached; rather soon the chromosome breaks down. In tumor cells, however, the telomeres do not become progressively shorter, due to the presence of an enzyme called *telomerase*. Active in the early embryo and germ cells, the gene encoding telomerase is usually turned off during the developmental process—effectively limiting the number of times particular cell lines will be able to reproduce. In cancers, however, the gene somehow gets switched on again—allowing the telomeres to be continuously repaired and granting unlimited reproductive potential to the cells that contain them.

The practical significance of this is obvious: we need to find ways to inhibit telomerase in cancer cells (to prevent their unbridled replication) and we need to find ways to activate it in, say, nerve and muscle cells, in order to allow such cells to reproduce so they can replace cells lost to the ravages of disease or aging. Hardly a week goes by without someone, somewhere in the world, filing for a patent on a drug or gene-therapy procedure intended to control telomerase.

Progress in the Reversal of Aging

Although it has been known for a long time that the aging process can be slowed down by such stratagems as caloric restriction of diets and consumption of antioxidants, the Holy Grail of aging research has always been the discovery of agents capable of *reversing* the chemical ravages of old age. It would appear that we are now beginning to drink the rejuvenating waters of that otherwise mythical cup. Research during the last decade or so has struck where aging hits hardest: the free-radical mediated glucose cross-linkage of collagen and other proteins.

It has been discovered—and now confirmed by dozens of experiments—that a simple molecule known as aminoguanidine can inhibit the formation of AGEs* [Advanced Glyca-

*[AGEs are formed when glucose reacts with amino acids, and accelerate cell damage.]

tion End Products]. Having more nitrogen atoms than carbons in its structure, aminoguanidine looks like it would more likely be a rocket fuel than a medicine! Yet it seems to be relatively nontoxic and very effective in blocking glucose cross-linkage of proteins.

There is even some indication that it can undo cross-linkage that has already occurred—thus actually reversing aging's chemical curse. While the jury is still out on this aspect of aminoguanidine's utility, it seems clear that compounds related to it will be found that will do this safely and without harmful side-effects. Although some clinical trials are now in progress that employ aminoguanidine as an anti-aging and antidiabetic agent (the high levels of glucose in diabetes accelerate the aging process), the compound is not yet approved by the Food and Drug Administration (FDA) for human use. . . .

Your Prospects for Physical Immortality

With reasonably good luck and careful management, you can survive to the year 2010. If you can live that long, scientific progress in the interim should have advanced to the point where it can keep you going until you're 140. If civilization still exists at that time, and if science has not been eclipsed by religion, you should be able to renew your lease as often thereafter as you wish. To an extent far greater than you may have dared to hope, it's up to you. You don't need help from the man who wears high-pointed hats and lace-fringed dresses. Barring accidental causes of death, immortality is within *your* reach.

No day goes by without another scientific paper reporting some progress in the war against aging, the war on death itself. In hundreds of journals, in over a dozen languages, the battle is enjoined. The New Day may dawn too late for some of my readers and for me, but not necessarily.

The Brave New World of immortality may very well number some of us among its citizens. The question "How will you spend eternity?" may assume an important new meaning very soon. John Donne's heroic "Death, thou shalt die!" may prove to be a boast more solid than skeptics have hitherto allowed!

But time is of the essence: time is the stuff that life is made of. The longer we delay our decision to do what already is possible, the fewer of us may hope to succeed where Ponce de León failed. We do well to remember the lines of Omar Khayyám:

A Moment's Halt—a momentary taste
Of Being from the Well amid the Waste—
And Lo!—the phantom Caravan has reached
The Nothing it set out from—Oh, make haste!
The Bird of Time has but a little way
To flutter—and the Bird is on the Wing.

> "Confronted with the growing moral challenges posed by biomedical technology, let us resist the siren song of the conquest of aging and death."

The Human Life Span Should Not Be Extended

Leon R. Kass

Leon R. Kass is a medical doctor and the Addie Clark Harding Professor in the Committee on Social Thought and the College at the University of Chicago. In the following viewpoint, Kass argues that efforts to extend the human life span through biomedical technologies will create numerous social problems and weaken important values that make life meaningful. Growing numbers of people living past one hundred may disrupt work opportunities, family structure, and cultural attitudes. In addition, living much longer lives would render life less interesting and reduce the human drive to pursue life with seriousness and moral excellence.

As you read, consider the following questions:
1. How do proponents of immortality research answer critics who contend that conquering aging and death will have adverse social consequences, according to Kass?
2. In the author's opinion, why would a life span increase of twenty years decrease life's pleasures?
3. How would immortality diminish human character, virtue, and morality, in Kass's opinion?

Excerpted from "L'Chaim and Its Limits: Why Not Immortality?" by Leon R. Kass, *First Things*, May 2001. Copyright © 2001 by the Institute on Religion and Public Life. Reprinted with permission.

If life is good and more is better, should we not regard death as a disease and try to cure it? Although this formulation of the question may seem too futuristic or far-fetched, there are several reasons for taking it up and treating it seriously.

Hormones, Stem Cells, and Genetics

First, reputable scientists are today answering the question in the affirmative and are already making large efforts toward bringing about a cure. Three kinds of research, still in their infancy, are attracting new attention and energies. First is the use of hormones, especially human growth hormone (hGH), to restore and enhance youthful bodily vigor. In the United States, over ten thousand people—including many physicians—are already injecting themselves daily with hGH for anti-aging purposes, with apparently remarkable improvements in bodily fitness and performance, though there is as yet no evidence that the hormones yield any increase in life expectancy. When the patent on hGH expires in 2002 and the cost comes down from its current $1,000 per month, many more people are almost certainly going to be injecting themselves from the hormonal fountain of youth.

Second is research on stem cells, those omnicompetent primordial cells that, on different signals, turn into all the different differentiated tissues of the body—liver, heart, kidney, brain, etc. Stem cell technologies—combined with techniques of cloning—hold out the promise of an indefinite supply of replacement tissues and organs for any and all worn-out body parts. This is a booming area in commercial biotechnology, and one of the leading biotech entrepreneurs has been touting his company's research as promising indefinite prolongation of life.

Third, there is research into the genetic switches that control the biological processes of aging. The maximum life span for each species—roughly one hundred years for human beings—is almost certainly under genetic control. In a startling recent discovery, fruit-fly geneticists have shown that mutations in a single gene produce a 50 percent increase in the natural lifetime of the flies. Once the genes involved in regulating the human life cycle and setting the midnight hour are identified, scientists predict that they will be able to increase the human maximum age well beyond its natural limit. Quite frankly, I find some of the claims and predictions to be overblown, but it would be foolhardy to bet against scientific and technical progress along these lines.

Conquering Aging and Death—A Worthy Goal?

But even if cures for aging and death are a long way off, there is a second and more fundamental reason for inquiring into the radical question of the desirability of gaining a cure for death. For truth to tell, victory over mortality is the unstated but implicit goal of modern medical science, indeed of the entire modern scientific project, to which mankind was summoned almost four hundred years ago by Francis Bacon and Rene Descartes. They quite consciously trumpeted the conquest of nature for the relief of man's estate, and they founded a science whose explicit purpose was to reverse the curse laid on Adam and Eve, and especially to restore the tree of life, by means of the tree of (scientific) knowledge. With medicine's increasing successes, realized mainly in the last half century, every death is increasingly regarded as premature, a failure of today's medicine that future research will prevent. In parallel with medical progress, a new moral sensibility has developed that serves precisely medicine's crusade against mortality: anything is permitted if it saves life, cures disease, prevents death. Regardless, therefore, of the imminence of anti-aging remedies, it is most worthwhile to reexamine the assumption upon which we have been operating: that everything should be done to preserve health and prolong life as much as possible, and that all other values must bow before the biomedical gods of better health, greater vigor, and longer life.

Recent proposals that we should conquer aging and death have not been without their critics. The criticism takes two forms: predictions of bad social consequences and complaints about distributive justice. Regarding the former, there are concerns about the effect on the size and age distribution of the population. How will growing numbers and percentages of people living well past one hundred affect, for example, work opportunities, retirement plans, hiring and promotion, cultural attitudes and beliefs, the structure of family life, relations between the generations, or the locus of rule and authority in government, business, and the professions? Even the most cursory examination of these matters suggests that the cumulative results of aggregated decisions for longer and more vigorous life could be highly disruptive and undesirable, even to the point that many individuals would be worse off through most of their lives, and worse off enough to offset the benefits of better health afforded them near the end of life. Indeed, several people have predicted that retardation of aging will present a classic instance of the Tragedy of the Commons, in which genuine and sought-for gains to individuals are nullified or worse, owing to the social consequences of granting them to everyone.

But other critics worry that technology's gift of long or immortal life will not be granted to everyone, especially if, as is likely, the treatments turn out to be expensive. Would it not be the ultimate injustice if only some people could afford a deathless existence, if the world were divided not only into rich and poor but into mortal and immortal?

Setting a New Life Span with Unclear Limits

Against these critics, the proponents of immortality research answer confidently that we will gradually figure out a way to solve these problems. We can handle any adverse social consequences through careful planning; we can overcome the inequities through cheaper technologies. Though I think these optimists woefully naive, let me for the moment grant their view regarding these issues. For both the proponents and their critics have yet to address thoughtfully the heart of the matter, the question of the goodness of the goal. The core question is this: Is it really true that longer life for individuals is an unqualified good?

How much longer life is a blessing for an individual? Ignoring now the possible harms flowing back to individuals from adverse social consequences, how much more life is good for us as individuals, other things being equal? How much more life do we want, assuming it to be healthy and vigorous? Assuming that it were up to us to set the human life span, where would or should we set the limit and why?

The simple answer is that no limit should be set. Life is

good, and death is bad. Therefore, the more life the better, provided, of course, that we remain fit and our friends do, too.

This answer has the virtues of clarity and honesty. But most public advocates of conquering aging deny any such greediness. They hope not for immortality, but for something reasonable—just a few more years.

How many years are reasonably few? Let us start with ten. Which of us would find unreasonable or unwelcome the addition of ten healthy and vigorous years to his or her life, years like those between ages thirty and forty? We could learn more, earn more, see more, do more. Maybe we should ask for five years on top of that? Or ten? Why not fifteen, or twenty, or more?

Immortality: A Bad Idea

One authoritative life-extension skeptic is Dr. Leonard Hayflick, a biogerontologist who earned fame in the 60's when he and Paul Moorhead debunked a longstanding belief that normal human cells in a tissue culture were immortal. Hayflick's work showed that normal cells die after about 50 divisions, indicating that they have a built-in mortality "clock." He doubts that science can beat the current maximum life span. Moreover, pointing at the social problems that superlongevity would bring—start with overpopulation—he just thinks it's a bad idea.

"Let's say a little white immortality pill does become available tomorrow," Hayflick says. "Do we really want people to have it? I can think of a lot of people—Hitler, Stalin, serial killers, rapists—that I wouldn't want to see live forever. We should leave these things to nature."

Alex Heard, *New York Times Magazine*, September 28, 1997.

If we can't immediately land on the reasonable number of added years, perhaps we can locate the principle. What is the principle of reasonableness? Time needed for our plans and projects yet to be completed? Some multiple of the age of a generation, say, that we might live to see great-grandchildren fully grown? Some notion—traditional, natural, revealed—of the proper life span for a being such as man? We have no answer to this question. We do not even know how to choose among the principles for setting our new life span.

Under such circumstances, lacking a standard of reasonableness, we fall back on our wants and desires. Under liberal democracy, this means the desires of the majority for whom the attachment to life—or the fear of death—knows no limits. It turns out that the simple answer is the best: we want to live and live, and not to wither and not to die. For most of us, especially under modern secular conditions in which more and more people believe that this is the only life they have, the desire to prolong the life span (even modestly) must be seen as expressing a desire never to grow old and die. However naive their counsel, those who propose immortality deserve credit: they honestly and shamelessly expose this desire.

The Blessings of Mortality

Some, of course, eschew any desire for longer life. They seek not adding years to life, but life to years. For them, the ideal life span would be our natural (once thought three-, now known to be) fourscore and ten, or if by reason of strength, fivescore, lived with full powers right up to death, which could come rather suddenly, painlessly, at the maximal age.

This has much to recommend it. Who would not want to avoid senility, crippling arthritis, the need for hearing aids and dentures, and the degrading dependencies of old age? But, in the absence of these degenerations, would we remain content to spurn longer life? Would we not become even more disinclined to exit? Would not death become even more of an affront? Would not the fear and loathing of death increase in the absence of its harbingers? We could no longer comfort the widow by pointing out that her husband was delivered from his suffering. Death would always be untimely, unprepared for, shocking. . . .

Thus it is highly likely that even a modest prolongation of life with vigor or even only a preservation of youthfulness with no increase in longevity would make death less acceptable and would exacerbate the desire to keep pushing it away—unless, for some reason, such life could also prove less satisfying.

Could longer, healthier life be less satisfying? How could it be, if life is good and death is bad? Perhaps the simple view is in error. Perhaps mortality is not simply an evil, perhaps it is even a blessing—not only for the welfare of the community, but even for us as individuals. How could this be?

I wish to make the case for the virtues of mortality. Against my own strong love of life, and against my even stronger wish that no more of my loved ones should die, I aspire to speak truth to my desires by showing that the finitude of human life is a blessing for every human individual, whether he knows it or not.

I know I won't persuade many people to my position. But I do hope I can convince readers of the gravity—I would say, the unique gravity—of this question. We are not talking about some minor new innovation with ethical wrinkles about which we may chatter or regulate as usual. Conquering death is not something that we can try for a while and then decide whether the results are better or worse—according to, God only knows, what standard. On the contrary, this is a question in which our very humanity is at stake, not only in the consequences but also in the very meaning of the choice. For to argue that human life would be better without death is, I submit, to argue that human life would be better being something other than human. To be immortal would not be just to continue life as we mortals now know it, only forever. The new immortals, in the decisive sense, would not be like us at all. If this is true, a human choice for bodily immortality would suffer from the deep confusion of choosing to have some great good only on the condition of turning into someone else. Moreover, such an immortal someone else, in my view, will be less well off than we mortals are now, thanks indeed to our mortality. . . .

Four Benefits of Mortality

How, then, might our finitude be good for us? I offer four benefits, first among which is interest and engagement. If the human life span were increased even by only twenty years, would the pleasures of life increase proportionately? Would professional tennis players really enjoy playing 25 percent more games of tennis? Would the Don Juans of our world feel better for having seduced 1,250 women rather than 1,000? Having experienced the joys and tribulations of raising a family until the last had left for college, how many parents would like to extend the experience by another ten years? Likewise, those whose satisfaction comes from climbing the career ladder might well ask what there would be to do for fifteen years after one had been CEO of Microsoft, a member of Congress, or the President of Harvard for a quarter of a century? Even less clear are the additions to personal happiness from more of the same of the less pleasant and less fulfilling activities in which so many of us are engaged so much of the time. It seems to be as the poet says: "We move and ever spend our lives amid the same things, and not by any length of life is any new pleasure hammered out."

Second, seriousness and aspiration. Could life be serious or meaningful without the limit of mortality? Is not the limit on our time the ground of our taking life seriously and living it passionately? To know and to feel that one goes around only once, and that the deadline is not out of sight, is for many people the necessary spur to the pursuit of something worthwhile. "Teach us to number our days," says the Psalmist, "that we may get a heart of wisdom." To number our days is the condition for making them count. Homer's immortals—Zeus and Hera, Apollo and Athena—for all their eternal beauty and youthfulness, live shallow and rather frivolous lives, their passions only transiently engaged, in first this and then that. They live as spectators of the mortals, who by comparison have depth, aspiration, genuine feeling, and hence a real center in their lives. Mortality makes life matter.

There may be some activities, especially in some human beings, that do not require finitude as a spur. A powerful desire for understanding can do without external proddings, let alone one related to mortality; and as there is never too much time to learn and to understand, longer, more vigorous life might be simply a boon. The best sorts of friendship, too, seem capable of indefinite growth, especially where growth is somehow tied to learning—though one may wonder whether real friendship doesn't depend in part on the shared perceptions of a common fate. But, in any case, I suspect that these are among the rare exceptions. For most activities, and for most of us, I think it is crucial that we recognize and feel the force of not having world enough and time.

A third matter, beauty and love. Death, says Wallace Stevens, is the mother of beauty. What he means is not easy to say. Perhaps he means that only a mortal being, aware of his mortality and the transience and vulnerability of all natural things, is moved to make beautiful artifacts, objects that will last, objects whose order will be immune to decay as their maker is not, beautiful objects that will bespeak and beautify a world that needs beautification, beautiful objects for other mortal beings who can appreciate what they cannot themselves make became of a taste for the beautiful, a taste perhaps connected to awareness of the ugliness of decay.

Perhaps the poet means to speak of natural beauty as well, which beauty—unlike that of objects of art—depends on its impermanence. Could the beauty of flowers depend on the fact that they will soon wither? Does the beauty of spring warblers depend upon the fall drabness that precedes and follows? What about the fading, late afternoon winter light or the spreading sunset? Is the beautiful necessarily fleeting, a peak that cannot be sustained? Or does the poet mean not that the beautiful is beautiful because mortal, but that our appreciation of its beauty depends on our appreciation of mortality—in us and in the beautiful? Does not love swell before the beautiful precisely on recognizing that it (and we) will not always be? Is not our mortality the cause of our enhanced appreciation of the beautiful and the worthy and of our treasuring and loving them? How deeply could one deathless "human" being love another?

Fourth, there is the peculiarly human beauty of character, virtue and moral excellence. To be mortal means that it is possible to give one's life, not only in one moment, say, on the field of battle, but also in the many other ways in which we are able in action to rise above attachment to survival. Through moral courage, endurance, greatness of soul, generosity, devotion to justice—in acts great and small—we rise above our mere creatureliness, spending the precious coinage of the time of our lives for the sake of the noble and the good and the holy. We free ourselves from fear, from bodily pleasures, or from attachments to wealth—all largely connected with survival—and in doing virtuous deeds overcome the weight of our neediness; yet for this nobility, vulnerability and mortality are the necessary conditions. The immortals cannot be noble. . . .

Confronted with the growing moral challenges posed by biomedical technology, let us resist the siren song of the conquest of aging and death. Let us cleave to our ancient wisdom and lift our voices and properly toast L'Chaim, to life beyond our own, to the life of our grandchildren and their grandchildren. May they, God willing, know health and long life, but especially so that they may also know the pursuit of truth and righteousness and holiness. And may they hand down and perpetuate this pursuit of what is humanly finest to succeeding generations for all time to come.

"[Cryonic suspension] . . . is the best avenue for eventual reanimation [after death]."

Cryonic Suspension Can Extend Life Beyond Death

Timothy Leary

Cryonic suspension is the process by which a person's body is treated with antifreeze agents after death and frozen in a container of liquid nitrogen. Those who elect to have their bodies frozen presume that advanced technologies will restore them to life at some point in the future. In the following viewpoint, Timothy Leary contends that dead people who undergo cryonic suspension stand a reasonable chance of being revived. According to Leary, in the next fifty to one hundred years, nanotechnology—the manipulation of matter molecule by molecule—will enable doctors to repair the damage to a person's cells and organs caused by cryonic freezing. As a result, the dead will be brought back to life with their memories and personalities intact. Leary was a medically trained psychologist recognized for his research with the psychedelic drug LSD. He died in 1996.

As you read, consider the following questions:
1. What reasons for hope does the author provide regarding the effectiveness of low-temperature preservation?
2. According to Leary, why is the brain easier to store in an organ bank than the heart?
3. What promise does nanotechnology hold for repairing the cells of people who have undergone cryonic suspension, in the author's opinion?

Pascal is famous for his street-smart, race-track advice: "Bet that God exists. You can't lose." Today's hot tip: "Bet that future genetic technology will produce options for rebirth. You can't lose." In other words, you may want to take advantage of the nascent opportunity to have yourself preserved for possible future action.

Although I have chosen to move on, I encourage others to consider cryonics as the only current reanimation technique wherein the continuous "I" returns with (possibly) memories intact.

I've been saying that cryonics is the second dumbest thing I've ever heard of, next to dying. Indeed, it's possible to consider the individual hibernating in cryonic suspension not dead on a theoretical level. This is, at the very least, a conceptual breakthrough of enormous proportions.

A Glorious Experiment

The medical and scientific communities would label de- and reanimation an "experimental procedure." It may not work. If you sign up with a cryonics group, you will be part of the experiment to see if it actually does.

There are reasons for hope regarding the efficacy of low-temperature preservation. In the 1980s, a two-and-a-half-year-old girl who had been suspended in freezing cold water for over an hour was successfully resuscitated by a heart-lung machine with no ill effects. Human embryos have been frozen, revived, reimplanted, and birthed. (Lawsuits proliferate on the issue of who gets custody of the child.) Several dogs have been brought to a near-frozen state, with the loss of heartbeat, and revived. Recently a successful brain aneurysm operation was performed on a human who was cooled to 15 degrees centigrade.

Mainline cryobiologists are skeptical about the likelihood of human revival, since they focus on the noticeable damage done by cryonic freezing. This cynicism, though, has to be seen as reflecting the blindness of specialists. They have not considered the possibility of subsequent damage repair. This hope is currently offered by the science of nanotechnology. There is every reason to assume that other theoretical and practical scientific procedures for undoing damage will follow. There's ample reason to believe that low-temperature hibernation (what some wags have called "corpsicles") is the best avenue for eventual reanimation.

The payoff for the cryonics organization occurs at the moment you pass over and they get to do their emergency response thing. Your cryonics team will jump into action, appearing at your bedside as swiftly as possible. Your body is put into an ice bath, where medications and a heart-lung resuscitator are used to restore breathing and blood circulation. This is done to prevent brain damage, which would otherwise occur due to lack of oxygen. . . . Then your blood temperature will be reduced to slightly above the freezing point of water. Finally, all your blood will be drained and replaced with an organ preservation fluid similar to that used for preserving donor organs during transportation. Your body is packed in ice, and off you go to the lab.

At the cryonics lab, the organ preservation fluids are replaced with an antifreeze agent. This will reduce negative effects of the freezing process on your cells. After a few days, your body temperature will be reduced to –196 centigrade, the temperature of liquid nitrogen. Finally, it's moved to a flask filled with liquid nitrogen. You will be stored head down (in case of accidental thawing you will lose your feet first). That's where you'll stay, doing a headstand and awaiting resurrection.

Or Just Take Along Your Brain

The option exists to freeze only your brain. The presumption here is that the technology will eventually exist to clone you a new body, or that your brain would be installed into the fully functioning body of a young person who has suffered brain death.

Brain preservation is cheaper than whole-body suspension. Focusing on the brain also allows for the optimal use of protectants during suspension. Cryonicists can concentrate all their efforts on just one organ rather than several. The brain is also a small mobile unit, easy to store. Just keep it on the mantle, or put it on top of the TV . . . but don't knock it over!

The idea of keeping someone's head in suspension pushes people's taboo buttons even more than whole-body suspension, which is one fun reason to *do* it. Saul Kent, one of the earliest supporters of cryonics and life extension, was arrested in a colorful case in which the head of his mother, Dora Kent, was taken off for cryonic suspension. The Los Angeles coroner's office decided that his mother had not been legally dead when her head was severed from her body and iced. The coroner wanted the cryonics company involved, ALCOR, to hand over the head, which would have effectively killed off Ms. Kent for all eternity. ALCOR evaded this. So the coroner's deputies, L.A. police, and a SWAT team invaded ALCOR's headquarters, removing all computing equipment, magnetic media, and prescription medications used for suspensions.

Eventually, after years of legal entanglements, the Dora Kent case slipped into oblivion. Dora's head still remains frozen, ready to tell us how it all looked from her perspective when she's reanimated.

Why Not Brain Banks?

We now have heart banks. These are places where healthy hearts of people who've undergone brain death are stored before being given to people with healthy brains who need hearts. We have kidney banks, liver banks, lung banks, pancreas banks, eye banks, skin banks, tissue banks, bone banks, and DNA banks. I suggest that there will soon be brain banks. In fact, the brain is much easier to store than the heart. The heart has all those muscles. And think of the kidneys with all that plumbing to maintain. The brain, on the other hand, has no mechanical parts. It has almost no hardware to worry about. The brain should be easy to store.

Now, if I donated my brain to a bank, I could suggest the parameters for the person I want to give my brain to. I want my brain to be put into a beautiful, young, black woman. Imagine a young healthy black woman running around with Timothy Leary's brain and memories. (I could finally get through immigration and into the United Kingdom!)

Memories Can Wait

Memories are most likely stored in molecular combinations in the brain. The question is how they can be recovered.

Nanotechnology and Cryonics:
An Ambulance to the Future

Natural molecular machinery is at the basis of all life. A peach tree contains intricate molecular machinery that rearranges the molecules in dirt, water and air into a peach. Artificial molecular machines developed in the next few decades will be able to do the same thing a peach tree does, but much more efficiently. . . .

The cell repair machines of molecular nanotechnology will not only prevent the natural causes of death, but most death by trauma as well. Artificial molecular machines can perform repairs far faster than the natural healing process. If an injury is so severe that it overwhelms the artificial healing process, the molecular machines can place the body into biostasis, halting all further damage until more help arrives.

The nanotechnology revolution could arrive within the next 15 years. . . .

Since the early 1960's, people have seriously discussed the idea of freezing those who die in the hope that future technology would be able to revive them and restore them to health. This process is known as cryonics.

Until the mid-1980's, the probability of cryonics being successful had to be considered as very slim. One problem was that no one knew what sort of technology would be able to revive the frozen dead. The hope of cryonics was based on faith that new technologies would continue to develop so that, perhaps 200 years in the future, the frozen could be revived.

Once the prospect of molecular nanotechnology became apparent, the grim prognosis for cryonics changed. We now know what technology (molecular nanotechnology) can be used to revive those in cryonic suspension, and we know that the cryonics organizations need only survive for the two or three more decades until the nanotechnology revolution. One cryonics organization has already survived for more than 24 years, and one man has already been cryonically suspended in liquid nitrogen since 1967.

At this particular time in the evolution of human technology, anyone who dies before the advent of nanotechnology will be losing centuries of healthy life. Burial or cremation eliminates the possibility of being revived by nanotechnology, but cryonics provides an ambulance to the future.

Colorado Futurescience, *Life Extension Manual*, 1999.

Neurologists claim that brain tissue that's suspended in liquid nitrogen can survive centuries without any signs of deterioration. The big hurdle in terms of bringing back brain function is freezer damage. While there's no reason to believe that a cure for freezer damage would violate any laws of physics, it seems that this repair is beyond the recovery capacities of the brain tissue itself. Therefore the possibility of full or partial restoration of brain function containing personality and memories rests on a technical intervention that can repair the damaged brain cells. Freezing yourself is basically a bet that a technology will evolve that can deal with this problem. Since it's reasonable to presume that there will be at least one or two generations of caretakers nurturing your frozen old head, the issue becomes whether it's reasonable to expect such a technology to be in place within the next fifty to one hundred years. The answer is a resounding YES! The reason for this hope is nanotechnology. . . .

Nanotechnology: Control over the Structure of Matter

For those of you who've been living in a cave or are understandably overwhelmed by info overload, nanotechnology is the inexpensive and complete control over the structure of matter. It's the manipulation of matter, molecule by molecule. The advent of nanotechnology will result in the human ability to create limitless amounts of any substance consistent with the laws of the universe.

A nanometer is a millionth of a millimeter. This is hundreds of times smaller than a wavelength of light. With nanotechnology, we're talking about the construction of mechanical devices of this scale. As we will see later in this viewpoint we're quickly working our way down toward having the ability to manipulate on that scale. . . .

A Brief History of Nanotechnology

Nanotechnology isn't just likely—it's more or less here now. But the road to nanotech has been littered with doubts and doubters. It all started with a talk by physics superstar Richard Feynman at the American Physical Society back in 1959 entitled "There's Always Room at the Bottom." Feynman asked, "Why cannot we write the entire twenty-four volumes of the *Encyclopaedia Britannica* on the head of a pin?" His argument revolved around the manipulation of atoms. It also presaged the basic argument raised by K. Eric Drexler [nanotechnology pioneer] in favor of molecular technology. That argument, in simple terms, is "If nature can do it, why can't we?" At the end of his talk, Feynman offered a reward to "the first guy who can take the information on the page of a book and put it on an area 1/25,000 smaller in linear scale in such a manner that it can be read by an electron microscope." A substantial portion of Feynman's audience of educated scientists thought that either Mr. Feynman had gone completely daft or that the talk was a put-on. Feynman would live long enough to pay the $1,000 reward and, in fact, to see IBM scientists spell out "IBM" with thirty-five individual atoms of xenon.

The race to "the bottom," the search for knowledge of—and control over—ever smaller particles of matter, continued across the subsequent decades. This rapid trajectory toward nanotech has been propelled by a series of unexpectedly quick successes.

In 1980, Hans Dehmelt, a physics professor at the University of Washington, stunned the scientific world when he trapped a single atom inside a complex system of lasers. In 1984, he trapped a positron.

In 1981, Drexler talked about designing proteins and building them to order as one of the most important steps toward nanotechnology. He admitted that this difficult problem could be decades away from resolution. In 1987, Du Pont scientist William DeGrado, explicitly influenced by Drexler's book *The Engines of Creation*, actually did the deed. He declared that protein engineering "will allow us to think about designing molecular devices in the next five to ten years."

The invention of the Scanning Tunnel Microscope in the early 1980s provided the tool needed for the manipulation of atoms. In 1987, Todd Gustavson, an eighteen-year-old Californian built his own in his father's workshop. It cost him $200. The specter of garage nanotechnology—nanopunk—is already an issue among the nano conscious. . . .

Bringing Back the Dead: Cryonics and Nanotechnology

Understand that nanotechnology, programming and building stuff molecule by molecule, is what nature does. So it makes sense that molecular machines can build cells (including brain cells) from scratch. Cell division demonstrates this. The development of embryos shows us that nanotech can build us organs. In the future, we'll have replaceable parts. Who wouldn't want to have a fresh young heart or a brand-new liver? Or who wouldn't like to repair a few brain cells? Especially us!!!

Neurobiology has given us the good news. Memory and personality are set in preservable brain structures. The marvelous two-hundred-billion-neuron network in our heads functions by molecular machinery. As Eric Drexler has put it, "Lasting changes in brain function involve lasting changes in this molecular machinery—unlike a computer's memory, the brain is not designed to be wiped clean and re-filled at a moment's notice. Personality and long-term memory are durable."

In other words, our future claims to individuality don't have to rely completely on our pretty faces. Memory and personality are contained in the way that brain cells have evolved patterns based on each of our experiences. Memory and personality don't expire the very second that you do. Biochemists and other scientists tell us that we'll be able to intervene in cross-linked structures and repair damaged cells. In all likelihood, presuming nanotechnology, we can come back at 100 percent, just like Woody Allen in *Sleeper.* All the recent explorations into neurology support the notion that memories, in fact, *can* wait.

"[Cryonics] promises everything, delivers nothing (but hope) and is based almost entirely on faith in the future."

Nano Nonsense and Cryonics

Michael Shermer

A small number of people in the United States have chosen to have their bodies frozen in a container of liquid nitrogen—a preservation process known as cryonic suspension—immediately after they die. Advocates of cryonics believe that in the next fifty to two hundred years scientists will have developed the technology necessary to restore these frozen bodies to life with minimal loss of memory and personality. Michael Shermer asserts in the following viewpoint that freezing and thawing a human brain destroys far too many cells for cryonics to work. The contention of cryonicists that nanotechnology will one day repair damaged cells through the injection of microscopic machines and resuscitate the dead is based on an overly optimistic vision of the future. Shermer is the founding publisher of *Skeptic* magazine and the author of *The Borderlands of Science*.

As you read, consider the following questions:
1. According to Shermer, how are cells damaged during freezing?
2. How is cryonics more like a religion than a science, in the author's opinion?
3. Why does the author assert that cryonics belongs to what he terms "borderlands science"?

Cryonicists believe that people can be frozen immediately after death and reanimated later when the cure for what ailed them is found. To see the flaw in this system, thaw out a can of frozen strawberries. During freezing, the water within each cell expands, crystallizes, and ruptures the cell membranes. When defrosted, all the intracellular goo oozes out, turning your strawberries into runny mush. This is your brain on cryonics.

Cryonicists recognize this detriment and turn to nanotechnology for a solution. Microscopic machines will be injected into the defrosting "patient" to repair the body molecule by molecule until the trillions of cells are restored and the person can be resuscitated. Every religion needs its gods, and this scientistic vision has a trinity in Robert C.W. Ettinger (*The Prospect of Immortality*), K. Eric Drexler (*Engines of Creation*) and Ralph C. Merkle (*The Molecular Repair of the Brain*), who preach that nanocryonics will wash away the sin of death. These works are built on the premise that if you are cremated or buried, you have zero probability of being resurrected—cryonics is better than everlasting nothingness.

Is it? That depends on how much time, effort and money ($120,000 for a full-body freeze or $50,000 for just the head) you are willing to invest for odds of success only slightly higher than zero. It takes a blindly optimistic faith in the illimitable power of science to solve any and all problems, including death. Look how far we've come in just a century, believers argue—from the Wright brothers to Neil Armstrong in only 66 years. Extrapolate these trends out 1,000 years, or 10,000, and immortality is virtually certain.

I want to believe the cryonicists. Really I do. I gave up on religion in college, but I often slip back into my former evangelical fervor, now directed toward the wonders of science and nature. But this is precisely why I'm skeptical. It is too much like religion: it promises everything, delivers nothing (but hope) and is based almost entirely on faith in the future. And if Ettinger, Drexler and Merkle are the trinity of this scientistic sect, then F.M. Esfandiary is its Saul. Esfandiary, on the road to his personal Damascus, changed his name to FM-2030 (the number signifying his 100th birthday and the year nanotechnology is predicted to make cryonics successful) and declared, "I have no age. Am born and reborn every day. I intend to live forever. Barring an accident I probably will."

Esfandiary forgot about cancer, a pancreatic form of which killed him on July 8, 2000. FM-2030—or more precisely, his head—now resides in a vat of liquid nitrogen at the Alcor Life Extension Foundation in Scottsdale, Ariz., but his legacy lives on among his fellow "transhumanists" (they have moved beyond human) and "extropians" (they are against entropy).

This is what I call "borderlands science," because it dwells in that fuzzy region of claims that have yet to pass any tests but have some basis, however remote, in reality. It is not impossible for cryonics to succeed; it is just exceptionally unlikely. The rub in exploring the borderlands is finding that balance between being open-minded enough to accept radical new ideas but not so open-minded that your brains fall out. My credulity module is glad that some scientists are devoting themselves to the problem of mortality. My skepticism module, however, recognizes that transhumanistic-extropian cryonics is uncomfortably close to religion. I worry, as Matthew Arnold did in his 1852 poem "Hymn of Empedocles," that we will "feign a bliss / Of doubtful future date, / And while we dream on this / Lose all our present state, / And relegate to worlds yet distant our repose."

Periodical Bibliography

The following articles have been selected to supplement the diverse views presented in this chapter.

Keay Davidson — "Biologists Seeking Longevity in a Pill," *San Francisco Chronicle*, February 19, 2001.

Mary Duenwald — "Discovering What It Takes to Live to 100," *New York Times*, December 25, 2001.

Abby Ellin — "Freezing Time: Plans for a Giant Cryonics Facility Are Heating Up," *New York Times Magazine*, April 22, 2001.

David P. Gushee — "How Immortality Almost Killed Me," *Christianity Today*, March 3, 1997.

Carl T. Hall — "Brave New Nano-World Lies Ahead," *San Francisco Chronicle*, July 19, 1999.

Carl T. Hall — "Happy 150th Birthday: Scientific Advances May Lead to Longer Lives and Many More Years of Youthfulness," *San Francisco Chronicle*, September 16, 1999.

Alex Heard — "Apocalypse Never," *Skeptic*, Summer 1999.

Alex Heard — "They Want to Live," *New York Times Magazine*, September 28, 1997.

Jeffrey Kluger — "Can We Learn to Beat the Reaper?" *Time*, January 21, 2002.

Richard Landau and James M. Gustafson — "Death Is Not the Enemy," *Perspectives in Biology and Medicine*, Autumn 1997.

David Lazarus — "Cryonics: The Movement to Store Bodies in Deep Freeze Is Feeling the Heat of Discord and Financial Problems, Placing the Industry on Thin Ice," *San Francisco Chronicle*, August 12, 2001.

Sherwin B. Nuland — "Immortality and Its Discontents," *Wall Street Journal*, July 2, 1999.

David Perlman — "Some Day, We May Not Look a Day over 120," *San Francisco Chronicle*, September 29, 2000.

Sharon Schmickle — "A Life Expectancy of 100? Not in Our Lifetimes," *Minneapolis Star Tribune*, February 19, 2001.

Frances Vaughn — "Conscious Aging: A Conversation with Ram Dass," *Connections*, September 1998.

Jim Wilson — "Cryonics Gets Hot," *Popular Mechanics*, November 2001.

CHAPTER 4

Is There Life After Death?

Chapter Preface

During brain surgery, thirty-five-year-old Pam Reynolds had a "near-death experience," or NDE, an event recalled by some people after a life-threatening accident or medical procedure. Technically brain dead during the operation, Reynolds's doctors had reduced her body temperature to 60 degrees and drained the blood from her head, stopping her heartbeat and breathing. As the operation progressed, Reynolds heard a sound that seemed to pull her outside of her body. She then remembers looking down on the operating table and being pulled up into a dark tunnel toward a blissful bright light, where her dead relatives beckoned her to join them. Reynolds wanted to go into the light, but she also wanted to come back to raise her children. Her uncle led her back through the tunnel and back into her body, and some time later, she regained consciousness.

The basic characteristics of Reynolds's NDE—the out-of-body experience followed by the sensation of moving through a tunnel toward a bright light—are remarkably similar to other accounts of NDEs, even those reported by children too young to have absorbed cultural expectations of life after death. Researchers of paranormal phenomena and some medical physicians cite NDEs as evidence that a person's "soul" survives physical death and continues in an afterlife. Says Diane Komp, a pediatric oncologist at Yale University Medical School who has listened to the accounts of dying children's NDEs, "I was an atheist, and it changed my view of spiritual matters. Call it a conversion. I came away convinced that these are real spiritual experiences."

Komp is not alone in her belief in a spiritual afterlife. According to a survey conducted by the National Opinion Research Center, 81 percent of the U.S. population believes that some form of existence awaits them after death. Not surprisingly, the majority of people who have an NDE lose their fear of death.

Some researchers, however, maintain that NDEs are triggered by biological responses in the brain. One hypothesis is that the brain releases euphoria-inducing chemicals in order to create feelings of separation from a traumatic experience.

Another explanation, asserted by Dr. Susan Blackmore of the Brain and Perception Laboratory in England, is that NDEs are caused by a lack of oxygen to the brain. As a consequence, the brain's visual cortex is stressed and begins firing randomly, generating the perception of a bright light or the feeling of being at the end of a tunnel. Perhaps most important, critics point out that people who have had NDEs cannot really say with certainty that there is life after death since they have not died.

An irrefutable, scientifically based explanation for NDEs may go a long way toward settling the question of whether there is life after death. Other as-yet-unexplained experiences that may uncover the mystery of life after death include reincarnation and communication with the dead. In the following chapter, experts debate and discuss these phenomena in their quest to answer whether life after death is a real possibility.

| *"Of* course *there is life after death. There is always life and we are always part of it."*

There Is an Afterlife

Susy Smith

In the following viewpoint, Susy Smith contends that human consciousness survives physical death as a "spirit" or "soul," which continues to exist in other dimensions of time and space. The author maintains that she regularly communicates with spirits who have left their bodies and moved on to "the other side." According to Smith, knowing that life continues after death may encourage people to live a better life, help ease of fear of dying, and comfort those who have lost loved ones. The author has written several books on psychic research, and in 1971, she established the Survival Research Foundation to develop scientific evidence for the survival of consciousness beyond death.

As you read, consider the following questions:

1. What did Einstein's theory of relativity lead some physicists to realize about the universe, according to Smith?
2. In the author's opinion, why is it of great importance to prove that there is an afterlife?
3. How does Smith communicate with the spirit world?

Excerpted from *The Afterlife Codes: Searching for Evidence of the Survival of the Soul*, by Susy Smith (Charlottesville, VA: Hampton Roads Publishing, 2000). Copyright © 2000 by Susy Smith. Reprinted by permission of the publisher.

It is easier to talk about the possibility of life after death than it was when I was a girl, a long time ago—I've got eighty-eight years behind me now. Then it was considered impolite to discuss such things as religion, politics or sex because you might cause an argument or hurt someone's feelings. And, of course, at that time scientists looked on religion as a delusion of the masses. Now television goes everywhere, so we are faced with evangelical preaching along with shampoo, Coca-Cola and furniture polish. And as for sex and politics . . . we just finished the nineties, for heaven's sake!

Mind and Energy

In 1905, a brilliant scientist named Albert Einstein came along with his relativity thing: $E = MC^2$. It was unintelligible to most of us, but it means energy equals mass times the speed of light squared. Physicists have since begun to open their minds a crack, realizing that with that statement Einstein pierced matter itself and discovered that everything in the universe is composed of energy or force. As modern physicist Michael Talbot writes in *Mysticism and the New Physics*, "There is no ultimate physical substance to matter." Einstein is also reported to have said, "Anyone who studies physics long enough is inevitably led to metaphysics."

Metaphysics implies a thinking process, doesn't it? And thus we are led to the awareness that mind—consciousness—is the controlling factor of all this energy. Author-lecturer Depak Chopra calls it "thinking non-stuff." Physicist David Bohm of Birkbeck College, London, says, "There's no sharp division between thought, emotion and matter . . . the entire ground of existence is enfolded in space."

Although this is difficult to comprehend at first, we can understand it when we think of the propeller of an airplane or the blades of an electric fan. When they are moving slowly, we can see them; when they are speeded up, we can't. So matter is energy moving so quickly—the speed of light squared—that we can only see it when it's slowed down. And the thinking property of matter, the animating force of life we call consciousness, is buzzing along so rapidly it is always invisible.

James, a spirit communicant I will tell you more about later, put it this way:

Natural laws, which govern all of the universe, do not change. You can use them even if you do not know what they are or how they operate. A good example of this is the force called electricity. Now, the power of thought is a natural law little understood or accepted by you people at the present time. Yet thought power is the strongest force in the world, and the sooner you accept this truth and put it into practice, the sooner you will benefit from it.

All matter can be controlled by thought, on Earth and everywhere else in the universe. If I had said this to you a century ago, you would have scoffed. But now the atom has been split and found to be composed largely of space and energy. Nothing but an infinitesimal amount of matter is discovered within the preponderance of space in each tiny atom; and this infinitesimal amount of matter is described by scientists as energy, force, or power controlled by consciousness.

The Evolution of Consciousness

About 1940, Stewart Edward White, a well known author of educational material for young people, began to receive what he believed was information through mediums from his deceased wife. She stressed particularly that "consciousness is the only reality and consciousness is in a state of evolution." Dr. Jonas Salk, many years later, referred to this as "metabiological evolution—the evolution of consciousness."

That is what many of our scientists today are saying: that all matter, including the human body, is composed of energy or force controlled by consciousness—which lives in everything, forever. Modern researchers are becoming aware that even though we are encased in matter, you and I and we actually exist as *consciousness* (or we can say "souls" or "spirits" if it won't distress the reader too much) and that our development as individuals of character and usefulness, of joy and love, is our most important function. "Love is the ultimate truth at the heart of civilization," says Chopra.

Rabbi Labil Wolk, interviewed in the *Providence Journal-Bulletin* in 1996, was characterized as "an explorer of Jewish mysticism." He stated: "Of course the notion of God in a mature sense lies in a more abstract area, an infinite source that underlies the reality of all existence not unlike what quantum physics is suggesting." Taking all this into consideration, wouldn't this overpowering consciousness, this energy that is eternally in everything—this invisible animating force of the entire universe and also the soul within us all—be God? An individual's consciousness or spirit or soul gradually becomes aware of its identity as an evolving human being as it develops from babyhood throughout life. At the death of the physical matter within which this awareness resides, the soul leaves, sailing forth into other dimensions of time and space. And continues to live forever as it grows in knowledge of its unity with God.

Ceaseless Energy

Coming to this point from our start with Einstein, we have Paul Davies, a mathematician and physicist in Australia, saying in 1983, "Science offers a surer path to God than religion." Won't it be a blast to eventually learn who is right!

Of *course* there is life after death. There is always life and we are always part of it. The world is composed of nothing but energy, which thinks and is real and possesses its own identity. Some believe that stones, trees and sand on the beach—all things—think, in one way or another. It's easy to know this about ourselves, because we are thinkers of thoughts and we know we are thinking. It's almost impossible not to be thinking all the time, even when we long for sleep and can't silence the chatterbox in our heads.

Maybe sticks and stones know they are thinking too, but we won't go into that here. Let's discuss instead how I came to be probing such deep subjects and why I think it is important to know that we continue to travel the road of spiritual development in an afterlife that awaits us all. While the physicists are doing this with their heads, I've been working on it experientially for many years. And still am—trying to prove it, that is.

Afterlife Codes . . . What Are They?

It occurs to me that readers might be wondering what codes have to do with the universal consciousness I've been talking about, and with the idea of life after death? I'll give you a hint. A code, or cipher, is secret writing meant to be understood only by those who have the key to it. In this instance it refers to a code that I have left in the computer of The

Susy Smith Project at the University of Arizona. I plan after my death to send "secret messages" (key phrases) that break the code, to mediums, psychics or any other persons who are able to receive them. An award of $10,000 is in my will for the first one who receives the message and breaks the code.

Spirit vs. Matter

The strongest positive argument against life after death is the observation of spirit at the mercy of matter. We see no more mental life when the brain dies. Even when it is alive, a blow to the head impairs thought. Consciousness seems related to matter as the light of a candle to the candle: once the fuel is used up, the light goes out. The body and its nervous system seem like the fuel, the cause; and immaterial activity, consciousness, seems like the effect. Remove the cause and you remove the effect. Consciousness, in other words, seems to be an epiphenomenon, an effect but not a cause, like the heat generated by the electricity running along a wire to an appliance, or the exhaust fumes from an engine's tailpipe.

What does the observed dependence of mind upon matter prove, if not the mortality of the soul? Wait. First, just what do we observe? We observe the physical manifestations of consciousness (e.g. speech) cease when the body dies. We do not observe the spirit cease to exist, because we do not observe the spirit at all, only its manifestations in the body. Observations of the body do not decide whether that body is an instrument of an independent spirit which continues to exist after its body-instrument dies, or whether the body is the cause of a dependent spirit which dies when its cause dies.

Peter Kreeft, *Truth*, 1985.

The concept is that if you hear it from me when I'm no longer on Earth, it should suggest that I've survived somewhere after death. Anyone else who wishes to leave a code may also put it on our computer. (Directions are on The Susy Smith Project Afterlife Codes Website: www.afterlifecodes.com.)

I think, and my spirit advisers agree, that it would be of great importance to the world to prove that there is a Hereafter. Knowing for certain that one was going to live indefinitely might encourage one to try to get off to a better start here. Accepting it on faith certainly has not been of any great value to the various religions, which have eternally fought over who is right in their beliefs. "Let's get some scientific evidence" has been my goal with all my research, and it will continue to be after I die.

The famous lawyer Clarence Darrow is reported to have said, "The truth is, no one believes in immortality." My communicant, James, who assures me he is William James, the Harvard psychologist and philosopher who died in 1910, wrote somewhat the same thing in *The Book of James*. He said:

> Many people do not ever think about the possibility of life after death. But most persons who think, think at one time or another about the subject—usually without achieving any answers that satisfy them. That is why they so often put the question aside, in order not to be embarrassed or confused by it.

But James has more to say:

> The truth is that your life has been for nothing unless you survive. Why should you go through all the difficulties and torments that everyone has to endure if there is no reason for it and no result from it, other than the perpetuation of the human race? Why should the species Man be continued at all, if he came from nowhere by chance coincidence and goes nowhere? To be extinguished like a light would mean that you remembered no more and suffered no more, it is true. But it would also mean that you nevermore knew joy and love.

Automatic Writing

The way I gained this type of philosophical information ostensibly from "the other side" was by what is termed automatic writing. Can you imagine how it feels to sit at your typewriter and have your fingers type information that your mind does not consciously instigate, that you don't even know? That is what I've been doing off and on for most of my life.

Naturally, I have questioned the source of the material, argued with it, and even fought with it. Does it really come, as it purports to, from surviving entities now residing in spirit dimensions of life? Or have I somehow tapped the universal unconscious—if there truly is such a thing? Might it be possible that my subconscious mind, with strange unfathomable powers, has gathered together brief bits from my (purposely) very limited reading of philosophical or occult literature; compiled, coordinated, reconstructed and embellished it with a great deal of additional information; and then poured it forth as automatic writing? To confound this theory is what three well versed Swedenborgians told me: a vast amount of the material written through me parallels exactly the accounts given in the eighteenth century by Emanuel Swedenborg, a Swedish metaphysician whose works I have never read.

In *Believe It or Not*, Robert Ripley said of Emanuel Swedenborg, "No single individual in the world's history ever encompassed in himself so great a variety of useful knowledge." The eminent scientist led a life largely devoted to studies covering practically the whole field of science. He traveled widely and was knighted by his queen for his achievements. He published volumes on mathematics, geology, chemistry, physics, mineralogy, astronomy and anatomy. This fantastic man gave up the study of worldly science at the age of fifty-six because he had become so psychic that he made daily trance visits into the spirit world—or so he believed. He wrote numerous works giving descriptions of the conditions he discovered there, and these became the basis for the Church of the New Jerusalem, which was founded after his death in 1772. Now without having the benefit of Swedenborg's information, since 1956 I have been receiving data very similar to his . . . which helps me accept my James's accuracy. . . .

Help from the Spirit World

To ask James to say a *few* words is a good joke between us. He doesn't mind my teasing him, though. His sense of humor was famous when he was on Earth and it's still going strong. Here's what he said, and to me it's quite encouraging:

This is your friend William James and I wish to congratulate you on the wonderful work you have done and will do in the future when you come over here. I have no doubt that someone will receive the key phrase that will break one of your codes or those of others who leave their codes with The Susy Smith Project. Those on Earth attempting to receive a secret message from the other side should sit in meditation every day. Who knows who might just get lucky. I will do everything I can to help all of you send your key phrases through when the time comes that you are here transmitting. We are already planning for mass cooperation. The words will be widely distributed here, and the thought power of many spirits will be centered on them. When one group stops concentrating on them, another will take over. This will be a major production circulating from spirits in all parts of the world in many languages. It may be difficult for you to understand the potential here. There are thousands available to help you people. Don't overlook our usefulness. We who continue to exist in this first plane after death want to be of help to those on Earth. And we will help. Keep your thoughts on a successful endeavor assisted by many spirits and we will be there for you. Don't underestimate us. Positive thinking all the way.

It is nice to contemplate the idea that people on both sides of the veil, those living on Earth and those who have passed on, will be making an effort to collaborate with all of us who are preparing and leaving these Afterlife Codes. At this point in my life, after all my years of research with my spirit friends, I am comfortable with their declarations of participation with us and do not find it difficult to accept them as reality.

Closer to Proving Survival of the Soul

Having one code or several codes broken by messages that seem to give evidence that they come from the spirit world could change the way people think and live on Earth. We cannot claim that this will prove the survival of the human soul after death, but it will certainly do more to indicate it than has so far been achieved. Many who have lost their loved ones and are grieving will be overjoyed to have a real indication that they will be reunited when they pass over. Those who are afraid of the looming nearness of death will no longer be panicked if they know there is a real likelihood that they will continue on in some other phase of existence. Certainly those who have felt their time on Earth wasted if they have not achieved the spiritual development they tried to attain will be encouraged to know what James has told us about the evolutionary progression of the human soul.

The possibility of something even close to scientific evidence that will help the bereaved feel confident that a spouse or a parent or a beloved child is not lost to them forever makes my heart smile.

| *"The death of the body entails the death of psychological functions, consciousness, and/or the personality."*

There Is No Afterlife

Paul Kurtz

Paul Kurtz is the founding chairman of the Committee for the Scientific Investigation of Claims of the Paranormal. In the following viewpoint, he asserts that there is insufficient scientific evidence to support the contention that consciousness can survive physical death. The case for a disembodied afterlife is based on dubious research that has been sensationalized by the media. In the author's opinion, communication with spirits, ghost sightings, death-bed visions, and other paranormal phenomena all have psychological and sociological, rather than spiritual, explanations.

As you read, consider the following questions:
1. What percentage of the U.S. population believes in life after death, according to Kurtz?
2. As reported by the author, what techniques do channelers use to trick audiences into believing that they are communicating with the dead?
3. How might psychological factors account for ghost sightings, in Kurtz's opinion?

W hat is the evidence for life after death? Can we communicate with the dead? That is, are we able to be in
touch with people who have died? Do they have some form
of existence, perhaps as "discarnate spirits" or "disembodied
souls"? This is an age-old question that is related to faith in
immortality and a very deep hunger for it. Although it has
been interpreted as "paranormal," it may more appropriately
be considered to be "paranatural" because of its religious
significance. Indeed, for the great supernatural religions of
the world—Christianity, Judaism, and Islam—belief in an afterlife and the promise of heaven are central.

Mass Media and Belief in the Afterlife

At present there is intense popular interest in these questions in the United States. It is stimulated by the mass media, at least as measured by the number of popular books,
magazine articles, movies, and television and radio programs
devoted to the theme. The films *The Sixth Sense* (with Bruce
Willis and Haley Osment) and *Frequency* are examples of the
prevailing interest, as are the best-selling books by James
Van Praagh (*Talking to Heaven*, 1997; *Reaching to Heaven*,
1999), John Edward (*One Last Time*, 1998), Sylvia Browne
(*The Other Side and Back*, 1999), and Rosemary Altea (*You
Own the Power*, 1999). Dan Rather on CBS, the Fox TV network, *Larry King Live*, and other talk-show hosts have devoted many uncritical programs to these claims. For example, the HBO TV network did a special last year, "Life
Afterlife," purporting to present the scientific examination
of survival. It interviewed dozens of people, all of whom
claim to have communicated with the dead, and several parapsychologists, all arguing the case for survival. Included in
this special were critical comments by two skeptics—one
more than usual! This is supposed to constitute a "balanced"
documentary, and it is typical of the state of American media
when dealing with paranatural or paranormal claims. There
are all too few objective programs examining such questions;
most favor a spiritual-paranormal interpretation.

As a result of a massive media onslaught, polls in the last
decade place the United States as number one in belief in life
after death in the democratic world, and higher than virtu-

ally all European countries. Two cross-national surveys conducted for the International Social Survey Program in 1991 and 1993 indicate that the United States ranked highest, along with Ireland and the Philippines, for those who believe in heaven (63.17% of the population), highest for those who believe in hell (49.6%), and highest for those who believe in life after death (55%). The US was lowest of twenty-one nations on knowledge of human evolution (44.2%), lower than Poland and Russia. Recent polls have shown the level of credulity growing in the past decade. In 1996 a poll conducted by Goldhaber Associates (at the State University of New York at Buffalo) indicated that 90 percent of Americans were either "religious" or "somewhat religious." A recent poll conducted for *Newsweek* magazine by the Princeton Survey Research Associates, based on a sample of 752 adults interviewed indicated that 84 percent of Americans said that God performed miracles and 77 percent said saints or God can cure people otherwise medically incurable. Paradoxically, the US is allegedly the most advanced scientific-technological society in the world.

A History of Life After Death Claims

What do scientists have to say about life after death? . . . Science has been investigating our ability to communicate with the dead for at least 150 years and it has attempted to discover empirical evidence in support of the claim. It began to do so with the emergence of spiritualism in the nineteenth century; more specifically, with the Fox sisters (Margaret and Kate), two young girls in Hydesville, New York (outside of Rochester), who in 1848 first claimed that they could receive messages from "the spirit world beyond." In their presence, there were strange rappings; people would receive answers to their questions spelled out by the number of taps. The basic premise was that human personality survived death and could communicate with specially endowed mediums. In the late nineteenth century and early twentieth century spiritualism swept the United States, England, and Europe. Thousands of mediums soon appeared, all seemingly capable of communicating with the dead. The most popular method of investigation was to try to communicate in a specially darkened seance room, wherein the discarnate entity would make its presence known by physical or verbal manifestations: table tipping, levitation of objects, ectoplasmic emissions, teleportation, materializations, automatic writings, etc.

A committee of medical doctors at the University of Buffalo tested the Fox sisters in 1851 and attributed their raps to the cracking of their toe knuckles or knee caps against a wooden floor or bedstead. The physicians did a controlled experiment by placing the girls' feet on pillows, and nothing happened. The great physicist Michael Farraday investigated table tipping (1852) and found that it was due to pressure exerted by the fingers of the sitters (whether voluntarily or involuntarily). Sir Walter Crookes investigated the most colorful mediums of the day, D.D. Home (1871) and Florence Cook (1873), and thought that they had special abilities of mediumship—though critics believe that he was duped by both.

The Society for Psychical Research was founded in 1882 in Great Britain by Henry Sidgwick, Richard Hodgson, F. W.H. Myers, Edmund Gurney, and others to investigate survival of life after death, among other questions. The American branch of the Society for Psychical Research was founded in 1885 by William James at Harvard. These researchers examined reports of apparitions and ghostly hauntings. It was difficult to corroborate these subjective eyewitness accounts and so these investigations focused on physical manifestations. There were numerous photographs of ghosts—which it was soon discovered could easily be doctored. Many famous mediums such as Eusapia Palladino (in Italy) and Leonora Piper (in Boston) were tested under controlled conditions in an effort to determine whether they possessed extraordinary powers.

Palladino was especially elusive, and the scientific community was split as to whether she was fraudulent. The Feilding Report was an account of sittings done in Naples (1909) by a team of scientists who thought she was genuine. Palladino was also tested in the United States at Harvard by Hugo Muensterberg (1909) and at Columbia University (1910) by a team of scientists; and in both cases the physical levitation of the table behind her and the feeling of being pinched by her spirit control (called John King) was found to be caused by her adroit ability to stretch her leg in contortions and to pinch sitters with her toes, or levitate a small table behind her. This was detected by having a man dressed in black crawl under the table and see her at work. A subsequent Fielding report (1911) also found that she had cheated.

Late in his career the famous magician Houdini (1874–1926) exposed several bogus mediums. By the 1920s the spiritualist movement was thoroughly discredited, because when the controls were tightened, the effect disappeared; skeptics insisted that if a person claims to be in contact with a spiritual entity, there must be some independent physical corroboration by impartial observers.

In the 1930s the survival question in science was laid aside. J.B. Rhine and others focused instead on psi phenomena [psychic events], again with controversial results, because scientists demanded replicable experiments by neutral observers, which were difficult to come by. In any case, whether or not psi existed was independent of the survival question.

Spiritualism Returns

In recent decades interest in the survival question has reappeared. This is rather surprising to skeptical investigators. No doubt this revival of interest is due in part to the growth of religiosity and spirituality on the broader American cultural scene, but is also due to the sensationalism of the mass media. I can only briefly outline some of the claims that had been made and the kinds of research that has been done. Most of this work is highly questionable, for the standards of rigorous methodological inquiry so essential to science seem to have declined drastically from what occurred in the early part of the last century.

(1) *Channeling to the other side.* Surprisingly, a new class of mediums, now called channelers, have emerged (such as James Van Praagh, John Edward, Sylvia Browne, and Rosemary Altea previously cited) who claim to be able to be put themselves into immediate contact with a dead relative or friend and to convey a message back from them. Thus, what we have are subjective reports based on the word of the

channeler that he or she is in touch with the departed spirit. There are two ways that this is done. First, there are "hot" readings, when the channeler may know something by previous research about the person being read. A good case of this is Arthur Ford, who did a reading of Bishop James Pike and claimed he was in contact with his son who had committed suicide. It was discovered after Ford's death that he had done extensive background investigation of Pike's son before the reading. The most common method used, however, is the skillful use of "cold readings" by the channeler. The public here is taken in by flim-flammery, and there is all too little effort to critically examine the claims made.

Conscious Life Ceases with Death

If there is one thing we can be virtually certain of, it is that there is no life after death (except in the minds of those who cannot come to terms with the prospect of their own annihilation). Science has revealed enough of the physicochemical basis of life for us to know that it is dependent on an awesomely complex network of chemical reactions and physical events. We have seen how the loss of some of that function, when we experience disease, diminishes our lives (Alzheimer's disease is a paramount example); it is absurd to think that any vestige of conscious life persists when the body has decayed. People long for immortality, but longing is not evidence. That we each appear to have a "soul" is not compelling, for the "soul" is nothing more than our sense of self allied with our sense of aspiration. Angels are extensions of the fairy stories we listened to as children and have as much existence. One can readily understand that whoever believes in God will believe in anything (indeed, if there is a God it would be valid to believe in anything), for God needs messengers and agents. However, angels are nothing more than remnants of our bewildered ancestors' beliefs that spirits lurked in the world.

Peter Atkins, *World and I*, 2001.

There has been a massive shift in the methodology used. If in previous decades scientists demanded some corroborative and/or physical manifestation of mediumship, today all rigorous standards of evidence and verification seem to have been abandoned. Psychologist Ray Hyman has shown how a psychic gives a general cold reading: if he throws out messages from the spirit world to an audience someone will usually emerge to whom it fits. Thus, he may ask, "Does anyone know a Mary, or a William?" And most likely a person will step forth who does, and then the reading proceeds, on a hit-and-miss basis. The skillful channeler simply has to have one or two lucky hits to mystify the audience.

(2) *Apparitions and other sightings.* Similar considerations apply to the epidemic of eyewitness testimonials that people have been reporting of ghostly apparitions, angels, and other ethereal entities. Such stories are pervasive today, since a tale once uttered may spread rapidly throughout the population; this is facilitated by the mass media and becomes contagious. If someone claims to see ghosts or angels, other people, perhaps millions, may likewise begin to encounter them.

What is so curious is that people who see ghosts usually see them clothed. It is one thing to say that a discarnate soul has survived, but that his or her clothing and other physical objects have survived is both amusing and contrary to the laws of physics.

The most parsimonious explanation that we have for this phenomenon is that it is in the eye of the beholder, satisfying some deep-felt need, a transcendental temptation or will-to-believe. The demand for independent objective verification seems to be ignored. It is puzzling why so many people will accept uncorroborated subjective reports, particularly when we find them unreliable. The death of a loved one can cause untold psychological trauma, and there are powerful motives, psychological and indeed sociological, for believing in their survival. Thus there are naturalistic psychological and sociological explanations that better account for the prevalence of such phenomenological givens, without the need to postulate discarnate beings or our ability to communicate with them.

Let me briefly outline two other areas of survival research, which at least claim to be more carefully designed.

(3) *Death-bed visions.* Osis and Haraldsson sent our questionnaires to doctors and nurses to ask them to describe the verbal accounts of death-bed visions of people in their last moments of dying. The question is whether these persons were able to communicate with departed friends or relatives

at the last moment or were merely hallucinating, as skeptics suggest they were. In any case, virtually all of this data is second-hand, and is influenced by cultural expectations that when we die we will meet people on the other side.

(4) *The phenomenology of near-death experience.* This is a very popular area of research today, widely touted as evidence for communication, and based on first-hand testimony. Much research has gone into this intriguing area by Raymond Moody, Elizabeth Kubler-Ross, Kenneth Ring, Michael Sabom, and Melvin Morse, among others. These extended phenomenological reports claim to give us evidence from the other side from people who were dying and resuscitated. There is an out-of-body experience, a vision of a tunnel, a bright light, a recall of one's life, and perhaps a meeting of beings on the other side.

Critics claim that the descriptive collage offered is of the dying process, and that in no case do we have reports of persons who have died (i.e., experienced brain death) and communicated with those on the other side. There are a variety of alternative naturalistic explanations. Skeptics maintain we are most likely dealing with psychological phenomena, where the person facing death has either hallucinations, has reached a state of depersonalization, and/or there are changes in brain chemistry and the nervous system. Some have postulated that the discarnate entities or divine beings encountered on the other side are colored by the sociocultural context; though proponents maintain that in spite of this there is a common core of similarities. Some have said that falls or accidents where a person thinks he is about to die, but survives, can cause analogous out-of-body experiences and panoramic reviews. Not everyone who is dying reports near-death experiences; and many people who are not dying report having them. Sleep paralysis and hypnopompic and hypnagogic dream states are factors in common out-of-body experiences. Ronald Siegel maintains that similar NDEs can be induced by hallucinogens. Karl Jansen has presented evidence that they can be stimulated by the dissociative drug ketamine. Various conditions can precipitate an NDE, such as low blood sugar, oxygen deprivation, reduced blood flow, temporal-lobe epilepsy, etc., and can lead to an altered state of consciousness. For skeptics, in no case can we say that the person has died and returns; what we are dealing with is the process or belief that one is dying.

Analytic philosophers have pointed out additional serious conceptual difficulties in the hypothesis that nonphysical beings are communicating with us—there is a sharp mind/body dualism here. Perhaps the real question is not whether there is sufficient evidence for "x," but the meaning of "x"; and whether we can communicate with "disembodied entities" who have a level of consciousness without sensory organs or a brain. Some have claimed that the communication is "telepathic," but the experimental evidence for telepathy is itself questionable.

Insufficient Evidence of an Afterlife

After a quarter of a century in this field of research, I find that eye witness testimony is notoriously unreliable, and that unless carefully controlled studies and standards are applied, people can deceive themselves and others into believing that almost anything is true and real—from past-life regression and extraterrestrial abductions to satanic infestations and near-death experiences.

What should be the posture of the scientific investigator about paranatural survival claims? Clearly, we need an open mind, and we should not reject *a priori* any such claim; if claims are responsibly framed they should be carefully evaluated. After a century and a half of scientific research, what are we to conclude? I submit that there is insufficient reliable or objective evidence that some individuals are able to reach another plane of existence beyond this world and/or communicate with the dead. As far as we know, the death of the body entails the death of psychological functions, consciousness, and/or the personality; and there is no reason to believe that ghosts hover and haunt and/or can communicate with us.

I realize that this flies in the face of what the preponderance of humans wish to believe, but science should deal as best it can with what is the case, not with what we would like it to be. Unfortunately, scientific objectivity today has an uphill battle in this area in the face of media hype and the enormous public fascination with paranormal and paranatural claims.

> "NDEs [near-death experiences] are bona
> fide spiritual experiences that have a
> reality that is independent of the physical
> brain."

Near-Death Experiences May Be Glimpses of an Afterlife

Kenneth Ring

Some patients who have recovered from life-threatening medical emergencies report having had near-death experiences, or NDEs, in which they left their bodies and traveled down a tunnel toward a blissful light. Many see those experiences as journeys of the "spirit" into an afterlife. Kenneth Ring asserts in the following viewpoint that NDEs are spiritual experiences that occur independently of the physical brain and cannot be accounted for by scientific explanations. NDEs provide evidence that life after death may be a distinct possibility, in the author's opinion. Ring is professor emeritus of psychology at the University of Connecticut and the cofounder of the International Association for Near-Death Studies.

As you read, consider the following questions:

1. According to the study cited by the author, what percentage of NDErs believed in life after death following their NDE?
2. How does the testimony of children who had NDEs lend authenticity to the author's claims that NDEs are a spiritual experience?
3. What does Ring conclude about the theories of critics who maintain that NDEs have natural causes?

For centuries, our Western civilization has inscribed in countless souls the frightening image of the Grim Reaper, that horrific symbol of death that forcibly comes to take us away—we know not when, we know not where. However, since the advent of research on near-death experiences (NDEs), the presence of a loving Being of Light, or the otherworldly Light itself, is fast replacing the Grim Reaper as the dominant image of death in our society. Despite this, one of the unfortunate things about the expression, the "near-death experience," is that it implies that this kind of experience only occurs when people survive a near-death crisis of some sort. This is not true. There are *many* ways in which persons experience other dimensions of reality without the necessity of undergoing a life-threatening medical emergency that culminates in an NDE. *Nearly* dying is *only one* reliable trigger of this experience. Other ways include meditation, mystical and spontaneous religious experiences, and out-of-body experiences that are not accompanied by any kind of near-death event.

NDEs and Belief in an Afterlife

From a strictly scientific perspective, studying NDErs who have been *nearly* dead provides, at best, *evidence* relevant to the possibility of life after death—it cannot *prove* what persons experience *after* irreversible biological death. Receiving testimony from the irretrievably dead could definitely settle the matter concerning the existence of life after death, but the irretrievably dead are notorious for never sending back their questionnaires!

One thing that *has* been demonstrated is that NDErs themselves do not need scientific proof in order to believe in life after death. For example, an Australian sociologist, Dr. Cherie Sutherland, conducted a study in which she asked NDErs about their beliefs in life after death *before* and *after* their NDEs. She found that *before* their NDEs, approximately 50 percent of them believed in some form of life after death. The remaining 50 percent either did *not* believe in life after death, or they had no opinion one way or the other. However, *after* their NDE, every single person *without exception* believed in life after death in some form. In my own contact with hundreds of NDErs, I've found pretty much the same thing.

Leaving the Body: A Spiritual Experience

For those of us who have not had an NDE, what follows is a very brief sampling of some of the research that supports the view that NDEs are bona fide spiritual experiences that have a reality that is independent of the physical brain.

One of the common features of the NDE is the undeniable sense that the individual's consciousness separates from the physical body. Psychologist Dr. Charles Tart, professor emeritus at the University of California at Davis wanted to test the hypothesis that "leaving the body" was possible. He found a woman willing to participate as a research subject who claimed to be able to leave her body at will.

The woman's experimental task involved reading a five-digit number that was written on a piece of paper that was placed on a shelf about six and a half feet high—well above what she could see from her laboratory bed. The woman was instructed to "leave her body," float up to the level of the shelf, read and remember the five-digit number, and then report the number the next day to Professor Tart. The woman was hooked up to electroencephalogram and electrocardiogram electrodes so that if she physically got out of bed to view the numbers, the experimenters would know it immediately.

The woman failed to read the number on her first three attempts, which is not that surprising given the novelty of the situation and the difficulty of controlling one's out-of-body state. However, on the fourth session, she correctly reported the number the next morning. The odds against this happening by chance are 100,000 to 1. Again, since her body was secured to the bed, this outcome strongly suggests that some nonphysical aspect of her consciousness—independent of her physical body—enabled her to successfully accomplish her assigned task. To the best of my knowledge, no one has yet offered a credible alternate hypothesis to explain the outcome of this experiment, apart from her somehow being able to read the researcher's mind telepathically, which, of course, would also strain a rationalist's heart to the breaking point. As you can imagine, those who believe in a strict materialistic model of the universe have extreme difficulty in accepting these results.

Another important study along these lines—but specifically with near-death survivors—was conducted by cardiologist Michael Sabom, who compared NDE accounts with actual medical records of what had taken place during heart operations. The NDErs' descriptions of what happened when they found themselves out of body while close to death—what was said and what was done on the operating table—very closely matched both medical records and the eyewitness testimony of nurses, anesthesiologists, and surgeons who were present during these operations.

Stages of the Near-Death Experience According to Kenneth Ring

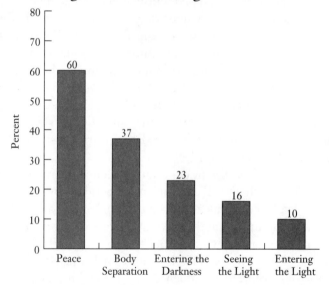

Susan Blackmore, *Dying to Live*, 1993.

It should also be mentioned that Dr. Sabom had a control group of non-NDE cardiac patients who were asked the same questions about what they would imagine would take place if they'd had such operations themselves. Their accounts were riddled with errors—for example, they described procedures that would only be found in highly dramatic "TV resuscitations," whereas such errors were *never* made by those who had actually undergone a heart operation and then reported they had witnessed it from an out-of-body vantage point.

The Blind, Children, and Deathbed Visions

Still on the subject of otherwise inexplicable visual perceptions that NDErs may sometimes report, I might mention here that one of my own research projects set out to discover whether NDEs ever take place in blind people and, if so, whether the blind report being able to *see* during these episodes. We found that most of our respondents, including persons who were blind since birth, claimed emphatically that in their NDEs they *were* able to see, not only things of *this* world, but things in the *other* world as well. In some cases, we even have independent evidence that their other-worldly perceptions—which they couldn't have known about by other means—were indeed accurate. Their testimony suggests that whatever limitations or handicaps we may suffer in this life are no longer operative when we are out of our physical bodies and exist in other dimensions. These findings bring a great deal of hope to many people concerning their freedom in the after-death state from handicaps that may have afflicted them grievously in their everyday physical life on Earth.

The study of NDEs in children also lends strength to the authenticity of the NDE as a spiritual experience by providing further evidence of its universality. This body of research shows, for example, that the accounts of very young children— some of them under two years old—were very similar to those of adult NDE reports. This is significant because these children could not yet be influenced by the culture-at-large or programmed by their parents or others with ideas from traditional religious belief systems. The existence of NDEs in very young children suggests that these and other similar spiritual experiences are intrinsic to the human experience. There is every indication that these NDEs or like experiences can happen to anyone at any age, even to the very young.

Another relevant source of evidence comes from a study entitled "Deathbed Observations by Physicians and Nurses" conducted by Drs. Karlis Osis and Dr. Erlendur Haraldsson. These researchers collected and analyzed what they called "deathbed visions"—experiences that were witnessed at bedside by over 1,000 doctors and nurses in a sample of about 35,500 patients who were very near death. Typical examples include a doctor who reports that a few seconds before a patient's death, the dying person says, with eyes closed, "Oh, the Light of God is so beautiful," or "Katie, you've come for me." Only later would it be confirmed by relatives that "Katie" was indeed a deceased relative who was very close to the person who had just died, but about whose death the dying person had not been informed.

Natural Causes Do Not Explain NDEs

Also in this study—and contrary to claims that paranormal experiences are hallucinatory experiences brought on by the side effects of narcotic-based medications—it was found that there were fewer reports of paranormal experiences from patients who were taking narcotics; such accounts were actually *more* common among those who were drug free or taking medicines known not to alter one's state of consciousness.

Since the beginning of NDE research, there have been those who have attempted to deny the reality of the NDE by regarding it as some kind of hallucination. Although such critics will admit that NDErs themselves almost always understand their own encounters as spiritual events that are, if anything, hyper-real, they are inclined to offer alternative theories that attribute NDEs to natural causes. Among the factors that tend to be cited by these critics are biochemical imbalances such as oxygen deprivation or metabolic toxicity; psychological defense mechanisms that serve our biological survival instinct's need to deny death; and genetically programmed neurological patterns that surface at the time of extreme biological crisis when the body's systems are closing down. Other natural causes cited to "explain away" the essential spiritual nature of NDEs include the limbic lobe syndrome, drug side effects, endorphin release, and sensory deprivation.

It is of course true that there *are* mediating biochemical, neurological, and psychological mechanisms associated with NDEs. But are these mechanisms *responsible for* and the *cause of* NDEs, or do they only sometimes *accompany* them? No matter how one views this indeterminate issue, we can at least conclude that, as of yet, none of these alternative theories can adequately explain how NDErs (especially blind ones!) can have verified, accurate out-of-body perceptions of objects and people in faraway locations where there is no rational possibility of any materially based mechanism affording this. Therefore, it seems safe to say that at the present time no neurological, biochemical, or psychological theory of NDEs, invoked singly or together, has been able to account for the kind of verified extraordinary events that occur during them.

Eroding the Fear of Death

I have attempted to share a brief overview of some of the evidence that indicate that NDEs are real spiritual experiences. Nevertheless, when I am with someone who is close to death, I don't cite research in a last attempt to convince the person to change his or her beliefs about life and life after death. However, if the person is open to exploring the topic and invites me to, I *will* talk with him or her about the Light that NDErs have described to me. This Light is, in effect, the heart in the body of the NDE. According to thousands of reports, in this Light is all love, total acceptance, knowledge, complete perfection, warmth, and a beauty beyond our ability to imagine. I've found that just speaking about this Light is often sufficient to reduce or even eliminate a person's fear of death. I've also found that many of our preconceived, traditional religious concepts of an eternal heaven and hell are not particularly helpful frameworks to dwell on in these life-leading-to-death situations.

With all the contact I've had with NDErs, their lack of fear of death, and the sincerity and conviction with which they talk of their experiences have helped to erode—if not completely extinguish—my own fear of death. This phenomenon is not unique to me. We now have research that shows that persons who are merely *exposed* to NDE accounts begin to experience many of the positive benefits of NDEs without having to have an NDE themselves. They develop a deep faith and trust in the inherent goodness of people.

Their love for God increases. They find their fear of death has diminished. They discover an increased ability to live more fully and more lovingly. And they are much more clear about what really matters in life—caring for other people and having love and compassion for all things.

In the future, I believe that the implications of NDE research—and the message of hope embedded in the NDE itself—will be widely accepted by our society and by the world as a whole. Not only will people continue to undergo NDEs, but more important, additional people will be pursuing near-deathlike experiences through meditation and other spiritual practices.

More of us will then come to know that it is only our ego's delusion about what is real that keeps us from experiencing the Light *in this very moment*, for the Light is the essence of what we ourselves are. Our challenge is to realize this and act on it *before* we die.

4

| *"The events of the NDE [near-death
| experience] must have naturalistic causes."*

Near-Death Experiences Have Natural, Not Spiritual, Causes

Barry F. Seidman

Following a life-threatening accident or health emergency, some people have reported undergoing a near-death experience, or NDE. During an NDE, patients recall floating outside their bodies and moving through a tunnel toward a bright light, encountering dead relatives and a God-like figure along the way. Survivors and parapsychologists view NDEs as evidence of an afterlife, where the "spirit" separates from the physical body. In the following viewpoint, Barry F. Seidman maintains that NDEs are caused by chemical reactions in the dying brain triggered by a lack of oxygen. The author is the director of the Center for Inquiry–Metro New York, an organization that promotes scientific naturalism over religion and spirituality.

As you read, consider the following questions:
1. According to the author, who introduced the phenomena of the NDE and implied that the strange occurrences were proof of the human soul?
2. What causes the "mind's eye" to perceive the tunnel and light during an NDE, in the opinion of scientists cited by the author?
3. In Seidman's opinion, why might the myths surrounding NDEs linger on, even though science will eventually offer a full explanation?

The yearning has been a uniquely potent one. Immortality; we want to live forever. We will invent—have invented—many ways to escape death's finality, at least in our minds, and have incorporated much of these into our myriad cultures usually under the guise of religion. It's not merely the fear of dying a horrible death, or going quietly in our sleep that disturbs us; it's the inconceivable idea that one day we will just cease to exist. It is an amazing enough feeling one gets after waking from an eight hour sleep without being able to recall even one dream. It is quite another feeling—one of desperate dread I'd pose—to contemplate going to sleep and never waking up to realize you hadn't dreamt . . . ever! Few of us are seriously concerned with how the world existed before we (you and I), came to be; but history is satiated with the emotional abyss that grows ever deeper with the realization that the world will, in all likelihood, exist long after we are gone. So, we've created myths. One of the most solid of these myths still being debated today is one which specifically tells of the everlasting desire for human existence beyond the grave.

The alleged evidence for such an "after life" most often is thought to be the proof that the religious "soul" exists. Unfortunately for those who depend on this myth, the nineteenth and twentieth centuries haven't been so kind. After living for centuries never questioning our most intimate hopes and ideas, there came a new kid on the block; mankind's most useful tool to understand the nature of things has been science, and science now has something to say about that pinnacle of "evidence" for the after life, the Near Death Experience (NDE).

What Is an NDE?

Twenty-three years ago, Raymond Moody—a medical clinician and philosopher—introduced us to the phenomena of the NDE, coaxing us to imply that the strange occurrences one had while near death was proof of the human soul. Since then, many psychologists, neuroscientists, and parapsychologists have investigated NDE's and some still hope to come to conclusions that will settle the debate once and for all.

What is an NDE? Close to death, many people across

many cultures and religions have reported certain odd sensations and "visions." Typically, they seem to float above their own corpse and see it from a bird's eye view. Some say that what is "floating" is the human soul. The person then sees a long tunnel with a bright light "beckoning" them to move through the tunnel into this light. Along the way they might encounter lost relatives and friends who have died, and God. The fact that persons of different religious up-bringing see "different" gods is—to the believer—to be expected.

These events are very powerful emotionally as one would suspect and those who have survived to live "again" often become happier and more stable-minded people. It is true however that some feel the worse for it—believers say they are so because instead of seeing God, they might have encountered Satan. So, what's really going on here?

"Something More" to NDE's?

Ian Stevenson, known for his lifetime of work dedicated to understanding Psi (i.e., ESP, Telepathy, and psychic powers), Parapsychologist Dean Radin, and Dr. Joanne D.S. McMahon of New York's Parapsychology Foundation are three of the front runners whom claim there's "something more" about NDE's than traditional science can explain. In particular, McMahon and Radin feel that one can't "take the NDE experience into the laboratory and expect to get accurate and true results."

McMahon is a strong advocate of Psi, of which she believes NDE's are a part, and feels that these extraordinary experiences are so multifaceted in their origins—covering such a wide range of physiology, psychology, and culture—that the "reductionism" science is known for simply misses too many explanations.

One such "missed explanation" that both Stevenson and McMahon quickly suggest is the "Psychic" element of NDE's. They feel that if one is truly dead or dying, he/she ought not to be able to describe items that they would not be able to "see" if alive. Some people for instance claim to see the goings-on on the street outside of the ER room they lie unconscious in. Others could recall—after resuscitated—the time on the clock in the next room! McMahon claims that this is possible due to some sort of "astral" body that leaves the body during such an "out-of-body experience." She wonders, "How then do you explain some of the psychic events that are incorporated within that whole constellation?"

McMahon and others seem to have come to a common ground amongst themselves. Scientists, they say, operate on too narrow of avenues, based on pin-point hypotheses, methods to prove or disprove these hypotheses, and then go on to the next subject confident that the mystery is solved. McMahon feels that in order to truly understand NDE's, one has to adopt more open-ended ways of thinking and come to grips that there may be no "real" answers because the NDE is too complex and subjective to discern.

Scientific Explanations

Today, unlike centuries, even decades earlier, we no longer tend to see mysteries that "ought to forever remain mysterious." In due time, many now believe, many such mysteries as NDE's will be solved as Sherlock Holmes himself might; by eliminating all the obviously wrong answers, and coming to provable conclusions—always testing everything along the way.

Dr. Susan Blackmore is on the front lines in the battle to understand NDE's. She has a Ph.D. in Parapsychology from Cambridge University in England and has spent years "really looking for Psi," and has found what she feels most educated in the method of science have found; that it doesn't seem to exist.

Blackmore has suggested that there are indeed sufficient and scientific ways to study NDE's that are not as narrow-minded as some might say. She explains that since one need not be dying to have an NDE—certain drugs can also elicit the experience—other methods for potential study are available. She also feels that researchers need not study a full-bloomed NDE in order to understand how it happens. "You can make theories about the experience which will have strong implications to things that do happen in the lab, and therefore test those bits and pieces in the lab."

Blackmore's approach is one of reason and critical thinking which are the prime ingredients involved in the act of doing science. "I feel that why so many people hate my view is that they think I am taking it [the NDE 'experience'] away from them. They think that meaningful, mystical and deep spiritual experiences have to have something to do with a soul or a spirit, which is independent from an ordinary mundane thing like the brain. These people are lurking about for 'something more'; they're simply looking in the wrong place."

Piraro. © 2002 by Dan Piraro. Reprinted by permission of Universal Press Syndicate.

Blackmore has allies. Dr. Barry Beyerstein, a psychologist from Simon Fraser University in Canada, argues that there is "no convincing evidence that consciousness can exist independently of an intact, functioning brain."

In as far as an NDE is a form of conscious—however feeble—the events of the NDE must have naturalistic causes.

Blackmore and Beyerstein agree: What happens is this. When the brain starts to die, functions start to fall apart one after the other, and the person experiences all sorts of strange phenomena. Neurotransmitters (chemicals that travel amongst the nerve cells of the brain sending and receiving signals), start firing irregularly and towards the center of the brain's visual cortex causing the "mind's eye" to perceive the famous tunnel and light of the NDE.

Mind's eye? It has been established that sight does not begin and end with the eye you see in the mirror. The optic nerve and other nerves in the vicinity can still detect visual signals and translate them to the brain for analysis.

Furthermore, the growing light that occurs as more and more transmitters fire causes the sensation of movement through this tunnel. If the person actually dies, the tunnel fades away. Since those who report NDE's obviously do not die, they perceive a return "out of the tunnel" as oxygen is returned to the brain and the transmitters perform their proper duty once again. This lack of oxygen is called anoxia. Scientists postulate that anoxia can also cause the hallucinations (of deceased relatives and friends), and sensations of bliss and ultra-relaxation many claim to have during an NDE. The fact that similar events occur over vast cultural and religious populations only goes to prove, scientists put forth, that NDE's are a natural human phenomenon that signifies the dying brain.

The Role of Memory

And there's more. To further understand the NDE, Blackmore postulates a theory that the brain subconsciously creates "mental models"—the most familiar of these is what we call "I"—so that it can organize and explain the world in a way that the conscious mind can understand. While the person is dying, the brain struggles to create the best "I" out of memory, and is why the NDE survivor feels the experience is "real." The "I" is constructed from memory and is not the "I" someone starts out with beforehand.

In memory, altered versions of yourself become your new

reality. Anything you hear or see—or have ever heard, seen, or even believed—can seem to be occurring during the NDE as in any other time in your life. You expect to see your family or God, as our culture has taught us, so you do. You, or your new "I," "sees" or hears things about you in the operating room—where doctors struggle to keep you alive—and you feel you are actually seeing them in real time.

Other phenomena can also be explained. For instance, the feelings of floating above your own body is also a result of the function of memory. Psychologists have long understood that we remember things from a birds-eye view. If the NDE's "I" is constructed from memory, it will "see" things from this same prospective.

As for the question which asks how someone blind from birth can "see" anything at all during an NDE, author Michael Shermer explains in his book *Why People Believe Weird Things*, that "memories of verbal descriptions given by others during the NDE are converted into visual images of the scene and then rendered back into words."

Similarly, one can understand how and why the infamous images of "ones life passing before ones eyes" can occur. According to Blackmore, the subcortical limbic system—a key area of the brain including the hypothalamus and the hippocampus, which regulate the sleep cycle, emotion, and motivation—and the temporal lobe of the cortex release chemicals like endorphins as higher brain centers are shut down subsequently flooding the brain with images from its memory sectors. She cites Canadian neuroscientist Michael Persinger, who has used an electroencephalogram (EEG), to study the temporal lobe. An EEG reads like an electrocardiogram (EKG) with "spikes" of activity showing up on attached monitors. Persinger measured the number of spikes per minute and found that the activity strongly matched the so-called "psychic experiences" of NDE's.

And, the Solution?

In time. From studies already in progress will come a better understanding of both the brain's functions, and the near death experience. The myths may linger on like those arguing against a much more proven theory, evolution, because people become intoxicated by mystical solutions to ordinary phenomenon, and indeed find enormous comfort in paranormal explanations because they can connect their unusually vivid experiences with their hopes of "life" eternal.

Dr. Blackmore admits that "people that believe in a life after death already have 'faith' that there is life after death and are somewhat happier and more able to copy."

Dr. Beyerstein warns, "I do not claim that everyone who believes dubious propositions will end up joining the Heaven's Gate folks, but I do agree with Voltaire who said we will only stop committing atrocities when we stop believing absurdities."

5

*"A rational person . . . can believe in
reincarnation on the basis of evidence."*

Reincarnation May Lead to Life After Death

Tom Shroder

Believers in reincarnation maintain that when a person dies, his or her soul will come back over and over again in different bodies. It is a belief that is widely held by followers of Eastern religions like Hinduism, Sikhism, and Buddhism. Tom Shroder contends in the following viewpoint that the research of leading reincarnation investigator Ian Stevenson offers convincing evidence that reincarnation is a real phenomenon, raising the possibility of life after death. Stevenson's cases primarily involve children who recall obscure details from the lives of deceased persons who lived in distant towns among different families. According to Shroder, short of a large-scale conspiracy to deceive investigators, many of Stevenson's reincarnation cases cannot be explained by the theories of skeptics.

As you read, consider the following questions:
1. In what manner does Stevenson respond to skeptics who claim that the lack of American reincarnation cases proves that some cultures are biased to believe in reincarnation?
2. According to Shroder, what does skeptic Paul Edwards seem to be admitting about Stevenson's cases if they could somehow be demonstrated to be honest and accurate accounts?
3. How does Stevenson defend his research against charges that his passion for reincarnation threatens his objectivity?

It is late, nearly lightless. Smoke from a million dung fires hangs in the headlamps as the Maruti microbus bangs along the narrow, cratered hardpack that passes for a paved road in the Indian outback. We are still hours away from the hotel, and the possibility that we will never get there looms as large as the absurdly overloaded truck hurtling toward us dead in the middle of the road.

Using every inch of the rutted dirt shoulder, we barely escape. I can feel the truck vibrate through the thin tin of the Maruti, smell death in the exhaust pumping from the truck's tailpipe, passing at eye level. And even in escape, there is no relief: We bounce back onto the road's pitted surface and immediately overtake a wooden cart moving at the lumbering gait of yoked oxen. Our driver, leaning on his horn, swerves around the cart and into a blind curve that I can only pray is not already occupied by a bus loaded to the dented metal ceiling with humans and farm animals.

I try not to think about the lack of seat belts, or the mere half-inch of glass and metal that separates the front seat from whatever we might plow into. Or the article I read that said fatal accidents were 40 times more likely on Indian roads than on American highways. I try not to think about dying 10,000 miles from home, about never seeing my wife and children again. I try not to think about absolute darkness.

Evidence Supports Reincarnation

But even within my bubble of fear, I am aware of the irony. Sitting in the back seat, apparently unconcerned about the mud-splattered torpedoes racing toward us, is a tall, stoop-shouldered, white-haired man, nearly 80, who insists he has compiled enough solid, empirical evidence to prove that physical death is not necessarily the end of me, or anyone else. His name is Ian Stevenson, and he is a physician and psychiatrist at the University of Virginia. He has been braving roads like this for almost 37 years to bring back reports of young children who speak of remembering previous lives, providing detailed and accurate information about people who died before they were born—people they say they once were. While I struggle with my fear of dying, he is wrestling with his own fear of annihilation: that his life's work will end all but ignored by his peers.

"Why," he asks for the third time since night has fallen, "do mainstream scientists refuse to accept the evidence we have for reincarnation?"

On this day, and for the past six months, Stevenson has shown me what he means by "evidence." He has allowed me to accompany him on two extensive field trips, first to Beirut and now to India. He has responded to my endless questions, and even allowed me to participate in the interviews that are the heart of his research.

The evidence he is referring to does not come from fashionable New Age sources, past-life readings or hypnotic regressions. It is homely and specific: A boy remembers being a 25-year-old mechanic, thrown to his death from a speeding car on a beach road. He recalls the name of the driver, the exact location of the crash, the names of the mechanic's sisters and parents and cousins, and the people he hunted with.

A girl remembers being a teenager named Sheila who was killed while crossing the road. She names the town Sheila lived in, plus Sheila's parents and siblings. When Sheila's family hears of the little girl's stories, they visit with her—in front of witnesses who say the girl recognized them by name and relationship without prompting.

From the time he learns to talk, a boy in Virginia named Joseph calls his mother by her name and calls his grandmother Mom. As he grows, Joseph begins recalling obscure events from the life of his Uncle David, who died in an accident 20 years before Joseph was born—and who has been rarely mentioned because of the family's abiding grief.

It goes on and on. In scores of cases around the world, multiple witnesses confirm that children have spontaneously supplied names of towns and relatives, occupations and relationships, attitudes and emotions that pinpointed a single, dead individual—often apparently unknown to their present families. Trying to make sense of these cases is what has involved Stevenson for almost 40 years. It is what we have been doing in Lebanon and India: examining records, interviewing witnesses and measuring the results against possible alternative explanations. And it is only now dawning on me, as we careen down a deathtrap of a rutted Indian highway, that I have no easy explanations for what I've seen, and no sure answer for the question the man in the back seat is asking.

A Rational Basis for Belief

If Stevenson is largely ignored by his mainstream peers, in some circles he is a scientific legend. His dogged collection of cases—closing in on 3,000 now—his meticulous documentation and cross-checking, his prodigious and scholarly publication have made him a hero to many people who would like respectable reasons to distrust the radical materialism of Western science. For his own part, Stevenson has reached this conclusion:

"I think a rational person, if he wants, can believe in reincarnation on the basis of evidence."

When I first came across mention of his work, in 1989, in a footnote to an article on hypnotic regression, I wondered if he might be the kind of wacko who also had a drawerful of fragments of the True Cross or a radio that communicated with a race of blood-red dwarves on the fifth moon of Jupiter. But reading further, I found that this was clearly not the case. A 1975 article in no less than the *Journal of the American Medical Association* said Stevenson "had collected cases in which the evidence is difficult to explain on any other grounds" besides reincarnation.

The article cited a book in which Stevenson had compiled his field studies, *Twenty Cases Suggestive of Reincarnation.* I visited a couple of book-stores and found nothing by Stevenson. The public library listed several volumes by him but could locate only *Twenty Cases.* The prose reminded me of some of the eye-crossing anthropology texts I'd read in college, but it was worth the read—the cases were compelling, even astonishing. Each had distinct particulars, each hinted at narrative enough for a novel, but all of them shared some essential aspects: A young child was said to have spontaneously asserted another identity, recounting details of memory and knowledge that appeared to conform to someone else's life.

Twenty Cases and a bookshelf of similar volumes Stevenson has produced are stuffed with elaborate examinations in which he sought to determine if the things these children said and the ways they behaved could be explained in any "normal" way. His methods are those of the social scientist, the detective, the investigative reporter. He methodically tracked down and interviewed firsthand witnesses to statements a child made, especially those uttered before any contact had been made with the friends or family of the deceased (in Stevenson's terminology, the "previous personality"). He cross-examined the witnesses, noted possible motivations for bias toward or against, and meticulously charted confirmations and conflicts in testimony.

The Case of Jasbir

Human beings have obviously survived death if they reincarnate. The best evidence for reincarnation, it seems to me, is set out, cogently and unemotionally, in the many books of Ian Stevenson. . . .

I am reminded of one of Stevenson's cases: the case of Jasbir, of Northern India. The boy was thought to have died of smallpox in the evening. He was left until the following morning when he stirred and was revived. He then showed a strange change of behaviour, said that he was the son of another person in another village, and wished to go there. He would not eat because he claimed to be of a higher caste than the family amongst which he found himself. He gave details of his former life as a young man.

All these details corresponded to those of a death in another village, fortunately reported to the family by a visiting lady who was recognised by 'Jasbir' as his Aunt. 'Jasbir' was later taken there and led the way round the village to his former home. Stevenson interviewed many witnesses in both villages and so produced exceedingly strong evidence that the facts were as stated. 'Jasbir' was asked what happened between his death and entering the other body. He said that he saw a holy man who advised him to go into Jasbir's body. He sometimes still saw the holy man in dreams.

Arthur Ellison, *Beyond Death*, 1995.

Stevenson has cases on five continents. Most he has found in cultures in which the idea of reincarnation is widely accepted—places like India, Sri Lanka, Burma and Lebanon, and among tribal groups in northern Canada. Many of those cases involve families who did not believe in reincarnation, or had other powerful motivations to disbelieve the claims of their children, or the children claiming to be their dead relatives.

American skeptics often find the apparent lack of cases in their own environment a powerful argument against crediting evidence from Uttar Pradesh or the Shouf Mountains. "Everyone wants a case in Iowa," Stevenson remarked at a dinner party in Beirut early in our travels. "Well, I'll give them a case in Iowa. They aren't as strong as the Lebanese cases, but they exist."

In fact, Stevenson has collected more than 100 accounts concerning non-tribal North American children who claim previous-life memories. As a group, the North Americans have fewer specific memories than the children in places like Lebanon and India. They tend not to talk about place or personal names as much, or at all, making identification of a specific previous personality unlikely. The only American cases Stevenson has found where children have said enough to clearly identify a previous personality and included verifiable statements about their lives are "same-family cases"—cases like Joseph's, in which a child remembers the life of a relative.

Such cases have at least two built-in weaknesses: There's a clear motivation—grief and the desire for the return of a beloved family member—for the child's family to unconsciously manufacture a fiction. And no matter how extensive a child's statements about a dead relative, there is no way of ruling out the possibility that he came by the knowledge from other family members.

Recalling Strangers' Lives

So the cases Stevenson has investigated most intensely are those in which it can be reliably established that the life a child claimed to recall belonged to a stranger, unknown to the child's family, or anyone the family had contact with. Cases like that of the girl who kept telephoning "Leila."

This was Suzanne, a middle-class Druze girl living in Beirut who believed that she remembered the life of a woman who had died undergoing heart surgery in Richmond, Virginia. Her parents told Stevenson her story: When she was 16 months old, she pulled the phone off the hook and said, "Hello, Leila?" into it over and over. Soon

Suzanne claimed that she was Leila's mother. By the time she was 2, Suzanne had mentioned the names of this woman's other children, her husband, and her parents and her brothers—13 people in all. At 3, she had recited portions of a funeral oration for the woman's brother. Ultimately, Suzanne begged her parents to take her to her "real" home, and they made inquiries in the Lebanese town the girl insisted she was from. There they found a family who fit the particulars Suzanne had mentioned.

And there they learned that minutes before undergoing her heart surgery, the woman in question had tried desperately to call her daughter Leila.

This family, including a sister of Leila's, confirmed much of what Suzanne had been saying: names, places, the funeral oration. Suzanne identified members of the dead woman's family from photographs. Though she was a child, she treated the dead woman's grown children as a mother would. She asked if their uncles, when they returned to Lebanon, had distributed "her" jewels to Leila and her sisters—which had been a deathbed request known only to the family.

Stevenson arrived on the scene after the two families met; any new statements the girl made about the woman's life would be tainted, because Stevenson would have no way of proving that the information didn't come from the woman's family. His recourse in such cases is to concentrate on obtaining firsthand testimony about what the child said before the first meeting, and how he or she behaved during it. The dead woman's relatives gave it, but grudgingly—they had been rocked by Suzanne's claims. That reluctance made their testimony all the more valuable, in Stevenson's view.

Suzanne's case is appealing in part because of its American connections: The woman died in Virginia, some of her children live in this country, almost everyone involved speaks English. But the fact remains that Suzanne was born in the hills descending into south Beirut, not in Rockville [Maryland,] or Woodbridge [Virginia]. Until someone else with memories of such detail and apparent veracity is documented in the United States, the relative weakness of American cases will inevitably suggest that the more persuasive foreign ones are somehow artifacts of a cultural belief in reincarnation.

Still, this view leaves several questions unanswered. Why, for example, do the American cases exist at all? Why are they identical, in form at least—the age of a child when the first statements are made, the type of statements and accompanying behavior—to the foreign ones?

And if a society's belief in reincarnation could be powerful enough to create hundreds of elaborate falsehoods, then why couldn't a society's disbelief be capable of suppressing or blunting genuine cases, if they existed?

As my interest in Stevenson grew, I read further. Beyond general, mostly uncritical mentions of Stevenson's work in literature dealing with New Age topics (one paranormal researcher compared him to Galileo), there was very little serious discussion of the meaning of his cases. But I did learn the basics of his biography:

Stevenson earned his MD from McGill University in Montreal in 1943, graduating at the top of his class. In 1957, at the age of 39, he became head of the department of psychiatry at the University of Virginia School of Medicine.

From there he began his research into reports of children who remembered past lives, and eventually gave up his administrative duties to become a full-time researcher of paranormal phenomena, his professorial chair endowed by Chester Carlson, the man who invented the Xerox process.

"Fatally Flawed" Research?

Apart from that early, positive review of Stevenson's research in the *Journal of the American Medical Association*, mainstream science had almost completely ignored him. I began to look through the indexes of more obscure journals on the scientific fringe, notably the *Journal of the American Society for Psychical Research* and, more recently, the *Journal for Scientific Exploration*. There, I finally found serious scholarly articles that critically assessed Stevenson's work, including some by researchers who had investigated similar cases themselves.

These researchers, psychologists and anthropologists, produced case reports almost identical to Stevenson's, although the conclusions tended to be somewhat more cautious. After investigating 10 cases in India in 1987, for example, anthropologist Antonia Mills wrote: "Like Stevenson, I conclude that while none of the cases I studied offer incontrovertible proof of reincarnation or some related paranormal process, they are part of a growing body of cases for which normal explanations do not seem to do justice to the data."

In 1996, Paul Edwards, a philosophy professor at the New School for Social Research in New York, published *Reincarnation: A Critical Examination*, an energetic attack. In his introduction, Edwards wrote:

"The writer most frequently criticized in this book is Professor Ian Stevenson of the University of Virginia. I should like to make it clear that there is nothing the least bit personal in these comments. I have never met Professor Stevenson . . . He has written more fully and more intelligently in defense of reincarnation than anybody else, and this is the only reason he features so prominently in my discussions."

In general, Edwards wrote, Stevenson's cases may look good in aggregate, but on close inspection are "fatally flawed." He quoted a former associate of Stevenson's as criticizing him for asking leading questions, conducting superficial investigations, taking insufficient account of the "human fallibility" of the witnesses he interviews, and reporting the cases in a way that makes them sound more impressive than they are.

"Which is more likely," Edwards wrote, "that there are astral bodies, that they invade the womb of prospective mothers, and that the children can remember events from a previous life although the brains of the previous persons have long been dead? Or that Stevenson's children, their parents, or some other witnesses and informants are, intentionally or unintentionally, not telling the truth: That they are lying, or that their very fallible memories and powers of observation have led them to make false statements and bogus identifications?"

Here Edwards was hammering at a central vulnerability of Stevenson's research: No matter how much evidence suggestive of reincarnation Stevenson accumulates, he cannot begin to say what a soul is, much less show how it might travel from one body to another.

On the other hand, in trying to make Stevenson's suppositions seem absurd, even Edwards was admitting that if these cases are not the product of lies, bogus identifications and fallible observations—if somehow they could be demonstrated to be honest and accurate accounts—then they would constitute legitimate evidence for reincarnation, even if we can't explain how reincarnation works. . . .

Convincing a Skeptic

The cases we encountered were every bit as difficult to explain away as he had advertised. As he readily acknowledges, no one of them could, on its own, rule out any normal alternative. But in many of them, the only way to account normally for what people were telling us was to hypothesize some massive, multi-sided conspiracy, either conscious fraud or some unconscious communal coordination among people from different families and communities with no obvious motive or clear means to cooperate in a deception.

It was also obvious that Stevenson wasn't ignoring contrary evidence or manufacturing support for his thesis. He was possibly even more energetic in pursuing a line of questioning that could puncture a claim than the contrary.

Ultimately, it was the accumulation of cases across culture and circumstance, all with multiple, independent witnesses matter-of-factly testifying to things that were inconceivable, that began to take a toll on my skeptical bias.

But what about Stevenson's bias?

On one of those interminable return trips on rutted roads unlit even by starlight, the evening fires encasing the world in an acrid smog, I asked him directly: Doesn't his own passion threaten the objectivity of his findings?

"Show me a researcher who doesn't care one way or another about the results, and I'll show you bad research," he said.

The car lurched off the road to avoid a truck burdened like an ox with sacks of grain overhanging its frame, but Stevenson didn't seem to notice.

"It's like line calls in tennis," he went on. "I care very much about winning my weekly games in Charlottesville, so I pay very close attention to whether a ball is in or out. It is a matter of honor to be scrupulously honest, so I'm not going to lie. But I'm not going to miss a call, either."

Besides, he said, his fondest hope is that other line judges will be called down from the stands to inspect the smudges in the clay and either endorse or dispute his conclusions. What was unbearable was the possibility that nobody would even look.

As he spoke of it, his steady imperturbability finally deserted him, the dangers awaiting outside the tinny van on the mayhem of India's roads vanishing in the overwhelming glare of the world's indifference.

Because one thing was certain. In this life, Ian Stevenson was running out of time.

| *"Reincarnation . . . cannot be reconciled*
| *with the body of scientific knowledge."*

Reincarnation Is a Myth

Paul Edwards

Paul Edwards is the author of *Reincarnation: A Critical Examination*, from which this excerpt was taken. Edwards is skeptical of researchers who claim to have uncovered substantial evidence that reincarnation—the soul's rebirth in new bodies after death—actually occurs, thus enabling life after death. In the following viewpoint, Edwards argues that the research of leading reincarnation proponent Ian Stevenson is fatally flawed. Stevenson has documented numerous cases of reincarnation where young children remember intimate details from the lives of deceased persons unrelated to them. According to Edwards, however, the children reporting memories of past lives most likely have been coached by their parents, relatives, and other guilty parties.

As you read, consider the following questions:

1. As cited by the author, what does John Beloff conclude about the rarity of reincarnation cases?
2. If Stevenson's reports are evidence for reincarnation, what "collateral assumptions" must they also be evidence for, according to Edwards?
3. In Edwards's opinion, why should the "servant" in the case of Jagdish raise doubts about the legitimacy of the boy reincarnation story?

Writing in the *Journal of Psychical Research* in 1986, James G. Matlock observed that, "[reincarnation researcher Ian] Stevenson's work is so far superior to any other in this area, and the body of evidence he has amassed is so intriguing, that the case for reincarnation rests largely upon it." It will hardly come as a surprise that Stevenson has become a hero to believers in reincarnation all over the world. It is difficult to pick up a book or pamphlet defending reincarnation and published in the last twenty-five years or so that does not refer admiringly to Stevenson's work. What may be surprising is that his work has been praised and some of it also published in respectable journals. Reviewing the first volume of his *Cases of the Reincarnation Type*, the *Journal of the American Medical Association* praised his "painstakingly and unemotionally collected cases from India in which the evidence is difficult to explain on any assumption other than reincarnation." Two of Stevenson's articles were published in *Journal of Nervous and Mental Disease* whose editor, Eugene Brody, proudly told the *New York Post* that he had received three or four hundred requests for reprints from scientists in every discipline. In the volume *Psychic Voyages* in the Time-Life series on the occult Stevenson's work is treated with great respect.

Among parapsychologists Stevenson's work has had a mixed reception. Scott Rogo and Professor [C.T.K.] Chari . . . are highly critical of it. The late Louise Rhine, the widow of the more famous J.B. Rhine, wrote a friendly but also highly critical review of *Twenty Cases Suggestive of Reincarnation*. John Beloff, the current editor of *Journal for Psychical Research*, is a guarded supporter of Stevenson's work. In a review of the second edition of *Twenty Cases* he writes that the book has "attained the status of a classic of parapsychological literature" and he concludes that "whether the idea of reincarnation appeals to us or not, Stevenson has made sure that, from now on, we can no longer ignore it." Beloff wonders why, since reincarnation cases are so rare that "one has to scour the world for them," one should not conclude that only some human beings reincarnate. In that case, I assume that for the rest us death is final. . . .

Let us now examine Stevenson's position and see whether

it stands up to criticism. . . . [A] formidable initial presumption against reincarnation [can be stated]. A believer in reincarnation is committed to a host of collateral assumptions the most important of which I will now enumerate. When a human being dies he continues to exist not on the earth but in a region we know not where as a "pure" disembodied mind or else as an astral or some other kind of "nonphysical" body; although deprived of his brain he retains memories of life on earth as well as some of his characteristic skills and traits; after a period varying from a few months to hundreds of years, this pure mind or nonphysical body, which lacks not only a brain but also any physical sense-organs, picks out a suitable woman on earth as its mother in the next incarnation, invades this woman's womb at the moment of conception of a new embryo, and unites with it to form a full-fledged human being; although the person who died may have been an adult and indeed quite old, when he is reborn he begins a new life with the intellectual and emotional attitudes of a baby; finally, many of the people born in this way did not previously live on the earth, but (depending on which version of reincarnation one subscribes to) in other planes or on other planets from which they migrate (invisibly of course), most of them preferring to enter the wombs of mothers in poor and over-populated countries where their lives are likely to be wretched. The collateral assumptions listed so far are implied by practically all forms of reincarnationism, but in Stevenson's case there is the additional implication that the memories and skills that the individual took over from the person who died and that are transmitted to the new regular body appear there for a relatively short time during childhood to disappear forever after.

If Stevenson's reports are evidence for reincarnation they must also be evidence for the collateral assumptions just mentioned. These assumptions are surely fantastic if not indeed pure nonsense; and, even in the absence of a demonstration of specific flaws, a rational person will conclude either that Stevenson's reports are seriously defective or that his alleged facts can be explained without bringing in reincarnation. An acceptance of the collateral assumptions would, to borrow a phrase from Søren Kierkegaard, amount to the "crucifixion" of our intellect.

It is of some interest to note that Dr. Eugene Brody, who published several of Stevenson's articles in the *Journal of Nervous and Mental Disease* and who appears not to see any significant flaws in Stevenson's investigative procedures, nevertheless refuses to accept reincarnation because it cannot be reconciled with the body of scientific knowledge. "The problem lies less in the quality of the data Stevenson adduces," Brody writes, than "in the body of knowledge and theory which must be abandoned or radically modified in order to accept reincarnation." "I am not yet ready," Brody concludes his review, "to regard the transmission of information or some aspect of 'personality' from a dead or dying brain to another brain-body in the process of conception or early development by unidentified means, over a significant time interval, as the most likely explanation for the cases which he has designated 'reincarnation type.'"

In a simplified form, the question before a rational person can be stated in the following words: which is more likely—that there are astral bodies, that they invade the wombs of prospective mothers, and that the children can remember events from a previous life although the brains of the previous persons have long been dead, or that Stevenson's children, their parents, or some of the other witnesses and informants are, intentionally or unintentionally, not telling the truth: that they are lying, or that their very fallible memories and powers of observations have led them to make false statements and bogus identifications.

Stevenson's cases read much better in summary than when one examines them in detail. He has admitted that all his cases, even the strongest ones, possess some weaknesses. I think that this is a gross understatement. They all have big holes, and they do not even begin to add up to a significant counterweight to the initial presumption against reincarnation. . . .

In [the following] I represent the critical examinations of two other cases by previous writers, both of which have been ignored by Stevenson as well as his associates. The first of these occurs in a review of *Cases of the Reincarnation Type, Volume One—Ten Cases in India* (1975) by J. Fraser Nicol. Nicol offers a detailed critique of two cases in the book under review. I will summarize the latter of these, because Stevenson himself regards it as "one of the best-authenticated" of all reincarnation cases. I agree with all of Nicol's strictures, and I will add some comments of my own.

Cryptomnesia and Reincarnation

Past-life memories are . . . considered evidence for survival, particularly for reincarnation. There has been evidence accumulated by parapsychologists where people provide accurate historical details when they describe "memories" of "past lives" while under hypnosis. This evidence, however, is more consistent with an alternative explanation—cryptomnesia. Melvin Harris describes this phenomena:

> To understand cryptomnesia we must think of the subconscious mind as a vast, muddled storehouse of information. This information comes from books, newspapers, and magazines; from lectures, television, and radio; from direct observation and even from overheard scraps of conversation. Under normal circumstances most of this knowledge is not subject to recall, but sometimes these deeply buried memories are spontaneously revived. They may reemerge in a baffling form, since their origins are completely forgotten.

There are numerous cases where information from past-life regressions has been traced back to such mundane causes upon further investigation. In fact, [according to John Beloff]

> In all the [past life] cases so far that have been elicited under hypnosis, either there was no such person as the one described or the character in question could have been known to the informant who . . . might consciously be quite unaware of the source of this knowledge.

Keith Augustine, "The Case Against Immortality," www.infidels.org, 1997.

The case concerns Jagdish Chandra who was born on March 4, 1923, in the Indian city of Bareilly. At the age of three and a half he suddenly claimed to have lived before as Jai Gopal in Benares. Stevenson regards the case as so strong because Jagdish's father wrote a brief account of the boy's memories for a newspaper before any contact had been established with the "previous" family in Benares. Jagdish's father, K.K.N. Sahay, was a lawyer and an ardent believer in reincarnation. After hearing the boy's recollections, he invited some "friends and members of the bar" to talk to the boy. He then published a letter in the *Leader*, an English-language newspaper, describing the boy's recollections and asking for confirmation if possible. A number of persons in Benares responded to Sahay's appeal. He then wrote additional letters to the press requesting the assistance of "some leaders of India to send their representatives," who would conduct the boy to Benares, which was about three miles from Bareilly.

Stevenson assures us that Sahay was a "person of the utmost rectitude," but in his letter to the *Leader*, he had made the false statement that he had no friends or relatives in Benares. In fact, he had a cousin and her husband living there, who could very well have told him about other families in that city. In 1927, Sahay published a pamphlet entitled *Reincarnation: Verified Cases of Rebirth After Death*. This pamphlet reproduces the following statement made by Jagdish on July 26, 1926, before a Bareilly magistrate:

> My name is Jai Gopal. My father's name is Babu Pandey. Our city is Benares. The Ganges River is near my house. The gate of the house is similar to the gate of Kuarpur in Bareilly. My brother was Jai Mangal. He was bigger than I am. He died of poisoning. . . . Babu Pandey keeps his money in an iron safe. It is on the left-hand side, sunk in the wall and high up. Babuji likes Rabri [an Indian sweet]. . . . Whenever Babuji washes his face, he massages it with clay. He has a phaeton. . . . He also has a motor car. My aunt wears gold bangles, . . . Babuji wears a ring. My aunt covers herself with a long veil. . . . The Ganges is nearby. My aunt makes bread. I wear a loin cloth when I take my bath, . . . Babuji has dark glasses. Babuji listens to the songs of a prostitute named Bhagwati.

Constructing a Likely Scenario

Most of what Jagdish said was found to be true. Nicol, however, points out that the magistrate asked no questions and evidently just wrote down what Jagdish said. It looks to him, Nicol goes on, like something learned by heart and recited on request. He also wonders if the Hindi word for "prostitute" is known among small children in India. Two months after Jagdish had made his first statements about a previous life, his father took him to Benares where large crowds had gathered. It will hardly surprise the reader that Jagdish was able to find the house of his former father, Babu Pandey, who denied being the father of Jai Gopal.

There are many gaping holes in this story. Stevenson tells us that when he was a young child, Jagdish was always under the protection of a servant or a member of the family. It is noteworthy that when Stevenson got to Bareilly, very long after this case had developed, he made no attempt to find the servant, assuming that he or she was still alive. Nicol asks how we can be sure that the servant may not have been the source of the boy's information. Nicol also regards the father or even the mother as possible culprits. My own impression is that the father was the guilty party. The following scenario seems to me a far better explanation of the events than any reincarnationist assumption. At the age of three Jagdish made some innocent remarks which the father at once twisted into reincarnation memories. The cousin and her husband who were living in Benares and whose existence Sahay had tried to hide supplied him with information about a person who had died at the appropriate time. This was Jai Gopal, and Jagdish before long came to believe what his father told him, that he had lived before as Gopal in Benares. The father then began his publicity campaign, terminating in the triumphant journey to Benares. None of this is farfetched if Nicol is right in his assumption that Jagdish's statement to the magistrate had been learned by heart. Jagdish himself probably repeated the story so often that he eventually came to believe it. Incidentally, there is a possible difficulty about dates. According to one account, Gopal died early in 1924 or at the end of 1923, i.e., *after* the birth of Jagdish.

Needless to say, I have no means of knowing whether the scenario just sketched approximates what actually happened. My construction is based on what Professor Chari[1] has revealed about the manufacture of reincarnation cases in India, and also what is known about religious or "holy" lying. . . . Religious lying [lying on behalf of a religious tenet,] is a depressing phenomenon, which has been discussed by many famous philosophers including Francis Bacon, Voltaire, and Hume. . . .

Chapter 23 of B.N. Moore's *The Philosophical Possibilities*

---

1. Professor Chari is an Indian philosopher who maintains that Stevenson's reports of reincarnation have no value because his research is collected in cultures where there is a deeply ingrained belief in reincarnation.

Beyond Death, an excellent book which deserves to be better known, contains a detailed discussion of the case of Sujith, which forms Chapter 7 of Stevenson's *Cases of the Reincarnation Type, Volume Two: Ten Cases in Sri Lanka* [1977]. Sujith was born in 1969 in Mt. Lavigna, a suburb of Colombo. He is reported to have started making statements about an earlier life in Gorakana, a small village seven miles south of Mt. Lavigna. Sujith mentioned a girl by the name of Kusuma in Gorakana who was able to connect some of his statements with her late uncle, Sammy Fernando. Sujith was taken to Gorakana where he reportedly recognized Kusuma, several of her relatives, and a number of other persons. From then on it was clear to the local believers that Sujith was, in fact, the reincarnation of Sammy Fernando. Moore shows in detail how Sujith could have obtained all this information by natural means. Moore also points out that Sammy Fernando died only a little more than six months before the birth of Sujith. Sujith's mother said that he was born after a seven-month pregnancy, something that has not been independently confirmed. Even if this is accepted, Moore remarks, the embryo was at least one month old before Sammy Fernando died. We therefore know that at one point Sujith was definitely not Sammy Fernando. If he later became Sammy, Moore asks, "what became of the individual who earlier was not Sammy: was he, too, reincarnated?"

In discussing this case, Stevenson refers to the critics who think reincarnation cases must, "accommodate to the current orthodoxy in biology." They regard the fact of Sujith's birth before Sammy's death as a disqualifying objection to the case. Stevenson tells us that a dispute arose on this point between Rationalist and Buddhists polemicists in the newspapers of Sri Lanka. "For me," Stevenson writes, "this controversy seemed concerned with a side issue. Cases of the reincarnation type, if accepted as authentic, challenge orthodox biology on assumptions far more important than the minimal length of pregnancy that can produce a viable infant." If this is so Moore comments, "proof of reincarnation would require disproof of orthodox biology, and thus would require evidence even more vast than that which supports orthodox bioiogy."

Periodical Bibliography

The following articles have been selected to supplement the diverse views presented in this chapter.

P.M.H. Atwater — "Near-Death Experiences of Children," *Fate*, June 2000.

Carl Becker — "The Meaning of Near-Death Experiences," *World and I*, March 1998.

John Elvin — "In Search of the Soul," *Insight on the News*, September 10, 2001.

Peter Fenwick — "Living to Tell the Tale," *UNESCO Courier*, March 1998.

Christopher C. French — "Dying to Know the Truth: Visions of a Dying Brain, or False Memories?" *Lancet*, December 15, 2001.

Leslie Alan Horvitz — "More Americans than Ever Embrace the Hereafter Now," *Insight on the News*, September 22, 1997.

Robert Hughes — "In Death's Throat," *Time*, October 11, 1999.

Brendan I. Koerner — "Is There Life After Death?" *U.S. News & World Report*, March 31, 1997.

Dyan Machan — "Bah, Humbug!" *Forbes*, March 6, 2000.

Kat Meltzer — "Change the Channel," *Skeptical Inquirer*, July/August 1998.

Bruce Moen — "A Voyage to Knowledge of the Afterlife," *Nexus*, April/May 1999.

Timothy E. Quill — "A View of 'the Other Side' Through Dying Patients' Eyes," *New York Times*, August 17, 1999.

Kenneth Ring and Sharon Cooper — "Near-Death and Out-of-Body Experiences in the Blind: A Study of Apparent Eyeless Vision," *Journal of Near-Death Studies*, Winter 1997.

Rami Shapiro — "Death & What's Next," *Tikkun*, July/August 1998.

John S. Spong — "Is Eternal Life Real?" *Human Quest*, March/April 2000.

Tony Walter — "Reincarnation, Modernity, and Identity," *Sociology*, February 2001.

Tony Walter and Helen Waterhouse — "A Very Private Belief: Reincarnation in Contemporary England," *Sociology of Religion*, Summer 1999.

For Further Discussion

Chapter 1

1. David Kessler argues that people who make their end-of-life treatment wishes known through the use of advance directives will have control over the circumstances of their deaths should they become incapacitated. Peter G. Filene contends that advance directives give people a false sense of autonomy over the dying process. Which author's arguments do you find more persuasive? Please explain.

2. According to Joe Loconte, extreme medical efforts to prolong life for the terminally ill should be rejected in favor of easing their emotional suffering through hospice care. Felicia Ackerman argues that treatment may be more important than emotional serenity to some terminally ill patients and considers the rejection of life-prolonging treatments a questionable aspect of the hospice philosophy. Which author do you find more convincing? Cite the viewpoints to support your answer.

3. Peter Rogatz states that legalizing physician-assisted suicide will not lead to a "slippery slope" in which vulnerable patients will be put to death without their consent. What reasoning does he provide in support of this assertion? In contrast to Rogatz's view, Wesley J. Smith maintains that proponents of assisted suicide want to expand the practice to include people who are not terminally ill. What evidence does Smith offer against assisted suicide? In your opinion, does the "slippery slope" theory appear reasonable or exaggerated? Please explain.

Chapter 2

1. According to Jerri Lyons, home funerals and other nontraditional funeral ceremonies are more beneficial to the grieving process than delegating death to the emotionally detached funeral industry. Joe Queenan argues that nontraditional funerals are simply another way for people to avoid the dreaded reality of death by turning it into a "celebration." Which type of funeral do you think is more likely to help participants come to terms with the loss of their loved ones and the inevitability of death? Cite the viewpoints to defend your answer.

2. Katherine Shear asserts that medical professionals can help manage the effects of intense grief, particularly for people who have experienced a sudden and violent loss. In Stephanie Salter's opinion, encouraging the bereaved to "manage" their pain ig-

nores the fact that grief is not an illness that can be cured with medication or even the passage of time. In your opinion, do you believe that medical treatment is a good idea for people struggling with grief? Give examples from the viewpoints to support your answer.

Chapter 3

1. Frank R. Zindler maintains that people should take advantage of the rapidly developing new technologies that will soon add decades to the human life span, if not actually lead to immortality. How does Leon R. Kass respond to Zindler's contention that extending the human life span is a worthy aspiration? What problems does Kass foresee stemming from large numbers of people living longer lives? Which author makes the stronger argument? Please explain.

2. Timothy Leary and Michael Shermer disagree over whether people who have their dead bodies frozen under cryonic suspension stand a chance of being revived. What is Shermer's main argument against cryonics? How might Leary respond to Shermer's criticism, based on your reading of his viewpoint? Explain your answer.

Chapter 4

1. Susy Smith contends that upon her death she will communicate with people on earth and send receptive individuals the key to a computer code she has left behind, thus proving the reality of an afterlife. Do you believe that Smith's experiment would meet the rigorous standards of evidence and verification which Paul Kurtz contends are essential to legitimate scientific research? Why or why not?

2. Kenneth Ring contends that near-death experiences (NDEs) cannot be attributed to natural causes such as oxygen deprivation, psychological defense mechanisms, or neurological patterns. Barry F. Seidman argues that natural causes are responsible for NDEs. Which author do you find most persuasive? Explain your answer.

3. Paul Edwards is critical of reincarnation proponent Ian Stevenson and argues that belief in reincarnation requires a disregard for the facts of biology and belief in a "soul." Tom Shroder maintains that Stevenson should not have to demonstrate what a soul is and how it might travel from one body to another. Based on the viewpoints, do you believe that Stevenson has uncovered legitimate evidence for reincarnation? Please explain.

Organizations to Contact

The editors have compiled the following list of organizations concerned with the issues debated in this book. The descriptions are derived from materials provided by the organizations. All have publications or information available for interested readers. The list was compiled on the date of publication of the present volume; names, address, phone and fax numbers, and e-mail and Internet addresses may change. Be aware that many organizations may take several weeks or longer to respond to inquiries, so allow as much time as possible.

Alcor Life Extension Foundation (ALEF)
7895 E. Acoma Dr., Suite 110, Scottsdale, AZ 85260
(480) 905-1906 • fax: (480) 922-9027
e-mail: info@alcor.org • website: www.alcor.org

Founded in 1972, ALEF is a group of individuals who have arranged to be cryonically suspended following their deaths. Cryonics is the preservation of clinically dead people at ultra-low temperatures in hopes of returning them to life with advanced medical technologies at some point in the future. ALEF's objective is to extend indefinitely the lives of its members. ALEF also conducts cryobiological research and maintains a speakers bureau. It publishes the monthly newsletter *Alcor Forum*, the quarterly magazine *Cryonics*, and several brochures and booklets.

Compassion in Dying Federation
6312 SW Capitol Hwy #415, Portland, OR 97201
(503) 221-9556 • fax: (503) 228-9160
e-mail: info@compassionindying.org
website: www.compassionindying.org

The Compassion in Dying Federation provides information and counseling to terminally ill patients and their families about intensive pain management, comfort or hospice care, and death-hastening methods. Its members believe that terminally ill patients who seek to hasten their deaths should not have to die alone because their friends and families fear they will be prosecuted if present. Compassion in Dying does not promote suicide but sees hastening death as a last resort when all other possibilities have been exhausted. It publishes several pamphlets on intensive pain management and on coping with the death of a loved one.

Death with Dignity National Center (DDNC)
11 Dupont Circle NW, Suite 202, Washington, DC 20036
(202) 969-1669 • fax: (202) 969-1668
e-mail: info@deathwithdignity.org
website: www.deathwithdignity.org

The DDNC promotes a comprehensive, humane, responsive system of care for terminally ill patients. Its members believe that a dying patient's choices should be given the utmost respect and consideration. The center serves as an information resource for the public and the media and promotes strategies for advancing a responsive system of care for terminally ill patients on educational, legal, legislative, and public-policy fronts. The DDNC publishes annual reports on end-of-life issues and posts numerous articles from journals and newspapers on its website.

Euthanasia Research and Guidance Organization (ERGO!)
24829 Norris Ln., Junction City, OR 97448-9559
(541) 998-1873 • fax: (541) 998-1873
e-mail: ergo@efn.org • website: www.finalexit.org

ERGO! works to achieve the passage of laws permitting physician-assisted suicide for the advanced terminally ill and the irreversibly ill who are suffering unbearably. It seeks to accomplish its goals by providing research data, addressing the public through the media, and helping raise campaign funds. The organization helps patients to die by supplying drug information, technique advice, and moral support via e-mail or postal mail or through the manual *Final Exit*. ERGO! also publishes a catalog of books and pamphlets on right-to-die topics.

Funeral Consumers Alliance (FCA)
PO Box 10, Hinesburg, VT 05461
(802) 482-3437 • fax: (802) 482-2879
e-mail: info@funerals.org • website: www.funerals.org

FCA works to promote the affordability, dignity, and simplicity of funeral rites and memorial services. It strives to provide every person with the opportunity to predetermine the type of funeral or memorial service he or she desires, including home funerals. It provides information on body and organ donation and on funeral costs, and it lobbies for the reform of funeral regulations at the state and federal levels. It publishes the quarterly *FCA Newsletter*, and *Before I Go, You Should Know*, and end-of-life planning kit that includes state-specific power of attorney and living will documents.

Hastings Center

21 Malcolm Gordon Rd., Garrison, NY 10524-5555
(845) 424-4040 • fax: (845) 424-4545
e-mail: mail@thehastingscenter.org
website: www.thehastingscenter.org

Since its founding in 1969, the center has played a central role in responding to advances in the medical, biological, and social sciences by raising ethical questions related to such advances. It conducts research and provides consultations on ethical issues such as assisted suicide and offers a forum for exploration and debate. The center publishes books, papers, guidelines, and the bimonthly *Hastings Center Report*.

Hemlock Society

PO Box 101810, Denver, CO 80250-1810
(800) 247-7421 • fax: (303) 639-1224
e-mail: hemlock@privatei.com • website: www.hemlock.org

The Hemlock Society believes that terminally ill individuals have the right to choose physician-assisted death to preserve their dignity and reduce suffering. The society publishes books on suicide and the dying process—including *Final Exit*, a guide to those who are suffering with terminal illnesses and considering suicide—and the quarterly newsletter *Timelines*.

Hospice Foundation of America (HFA)

2001 S St. NW, Suite 300, Washington, DC 20009
(800) 854-3402 • fax: (202) 638-5312
e-mail: jon@hospicefoundation.org
website: www.hospicefoundation.org

HFA advocates hospice care as an important enhancement to the American system of end-of-life care for the terminally ill. The foundation conducts research and public education programs to raise awareness of hospice programs and assist those coping with death and the process of grief. HFA publishes the monthly e-mail newsletter *HFA E-Newsletter*, and *Journeys*, a monthly newsletter to help in bereavement.

International Association for Near-Death Studies (IANDS)

PO Box 502, East Windsor Hill, CT 06028-0502
(860) 644-5216 • fax: (860) 644-5759
e-mail: office@iands.org • website: www.iands.org

IANDS is a worldwide organization of scientists, scholars, and others who are interested in or who have had near-death experiences. It supports the scientific study of near-death experiences and their implications, fosters communication among researchers on this topic, and sponsors support groups in which people can discuss their near-death experiences. The association publishes the quarterly newsletter *Vital Signs.*

International Task Force on Euthanasia and Assisted Suicide
PO Box 760, Steubenville, OH 43952
(740) 282-3810
e-mail: www.internationaltaskforce.org

The International Task Force on Euthanasia and Assisted Suicide is a group of individuals who oppose euthanasia. The group works to provide information on euthanasia and related end-of-life issues, to promote the right of all persons to be treated with respect, dignity, and compassion, and to combat attitudes, programs, and policies that its members believe threaten the lives of those who are medically vulnerable. It conducts seminars and workshops and publishes several books on assisted suicide including *Forced Exit: The Slippery Slope from Assisted Suicide to Legalized Murder,* in addition to the bimonthly newsletter *Update.*

National Hospice Foundation (NHF)
1700 Diagonal Rd., Suite 625, Alexandria, VA 22314
(703) 516-4928 • fax: (703) 837-1233
e-mail: nhf@nhpco.org • website: www.hospiceinfo.org

NHF works to educate the public about the benefits of hospice care for the terminally ill and their families. It promotes the idea that, with the proper care and pain medication, the terminally ill can live out their lives comfortably and in the company of their families. It publishes consumer brochures on hospice care including *Communicating Your End-of-Life Wishes* and *Hospice Care: A Consumer's Guide to Selecting a Hospice Program.*

Partnership for Caring (PFC)
1620 Eye St. NW, Suite 202, Washington, DC 20006
(202) 296-8071 • fax: (202) 296-8352
e-mail: pfc@partnershipforcaring.org
website: www.partnershipforcaring.org

PFC educates professionals and the public on the legal, ethical, and psychological consequences of decisions concerning the terminally ill. The partnership advocates the use of Advance Directives such as living wills to give patients more control over their end-of-life care. PFC publishes the quarterly *End-of-Life Law Digest,* which tracks state and federal laws affecting end-of-life care.

Bibliography of Books

Susan J. Blackmore   *Dying to Live: Near-Death Experiences.* Amherst, NY: Prometheus Books, 1993.

Herb Bowie   *Why Die? A Beginner's Guide to Living Forever.* Scottsdale, AZ: PowerSurge Publishing, 1998.

Mary Bradbury   *Representations of Death: A Social Psychological Perspective.* New York: Routledge, 1999.

Ira Byock   *Dying Well: The Prospect for Growth at the End of Life.* New York: Riverhead Books, 1997.

Maggie Callanan and Patricia Kelley   *Final Gifts: Understanding the Special Awareness, Needs, and Communications of the Dying.* New York: Bantam Books, 1997.

William R. Clark   *A Means to an End: The Biological Basis of Aging and Death.* New York: Oxford University Press, 2002.

Raphael Cohen-Almagor   *The Right to Die with Dignity: An Argument in Ethics, Medicine, and Law.* Piscataway, NJ: Rutgers University Press, 2001.

Dan Cohn-Sherbok and Christopher Lewis, eds.   *Beyond Death: Theological and Philosophical Reflections on Life After Death.* New York: St. Martin's Press, 1995.

Betty J. Eadie   *Embraced by the Light: Personal Triumphs over Loss and Grief.* Everett, WA: Ojinjinkta Publishing, 2002.

Paul Edwards   *Reincarnation: A Critical Examination.* Amherst, NY: Prometheus Books, 2001.

R.E. Erwin   *Reasons for the Fear of Death.* Lanham, MD: Rowman and Littlefield, 2002.

Peter G. Filene   *In the Arms of Others: A Cultural History of the Right-to-Die in America.* Chicago: Ivan R. Dee, 1998.

Louise Harmon   *Fragments on the Deathwatch.* Boston: Beacon Press, 1998.

Leonard Hayflick   *How and Why We Age.* New York: Ballantine Books, 1996.

Donald Heinz   *The Last Passage: Recovering a Death of Our Own.* New York: Oxford University Press, 1999.

Herbert Hendin   *Seduced by Death: Doctors, Patients, and Assisted Suicide.* New York: W.W. Norton, 1998.

Gregg Horowitz   *Sustaining Loss.* Stanford, CA: Stanford University Press, 2001.

John Keown   *Regulating Voluntary Euthanasia.* New York:
                           Cambridge University Press, 2002.

David Kessler   *The Rights of the Dying: A Companion for Life's
                           Final Moments.* New York: HarperCollins, 1997.

Elisabeth Kubler-Ross   *On Death & Dying.* New York: Simon and
                           Schuster, 1997.

David Kuhl   *What Dying People Want: Practical Wisdom for the
                           End of Life.* New York: Public Affairs, 2002.

Philippe Labro,   *Dark Tunnel, White Light: My Journey to Death
trans. by   and Beyond.* New York: Kodansha International,
Linda Coverdale   1997

Timothy Leary with   *Design for Dying.* San Francisco: HarperEdge,
R.U. Sirius   1997.

Erich H. Loewy and   *The Ethics of Terminal Care: Orchestrating the End
Roberta Springer   of Life.* New York: Kluwer Academic/Plenum
Loewy   Publishers, 2000.

Jessica Mitford   *The American Way of Death Revisited.* New York:
                           Vintage Books, 2000.

Raymond A. Moody   *Life After Life: The Investigation of a Phenomenon,
                           Survival of Bodily Death.* New York: Walker,
                           1988.

Ernest Morgan et al.   *Dealing Creatively with Death: A Manual of
                           Death Education and Simple Burial.* Hinesburg,
                           VT: Upper Access, 2001.

Christine Quigley   *Modern Mummies: The Preservation of the Human
                           Body in the Twentieth Century.* Jefferson, NC:
                           McFarland, 1998.

Renee C. Rebman   *Euthanasia and the Right to Die: A Pro/Con Issue.*
                           Berkeley Heights, NJ: Enslow, 2002.

Kenneth Ring and   *Lessons from the Light: What We Can Learn from
Evelyn Elsaesser   the Near-Death Experience.* Portsmouth, NH:
Valarino   Moment Point Press, 1998.

Kenneth Ring and   *Life at Death: A Scientific Investigation of the
Raymond A. Moody Jr.   Near-Death Experience.* New York: Quill, 1982.

Barbara Roberts   *Death Without Denial, Grief Without Apology: A
                           Guide for Facing Death & Loss.* Troutdale, OR:
                           NewSage Press, 2002.

Eliot Jay Rosen, ed.   *Experiencing the Soul: Before Birth, During Life,
                           After Death.* Carlsbad, CA: Hay House, 1998.

Clive Seale   *Constructing Death.* Cambridge, UK: Cam-
                           bridge University Press, 1998.

Susy Smith   *Afterlife Codes.* Charlottesville, VA: Hampton
                           Roads Publishing, 2000.

Margaret A. Somerville	*Death Talk: The Case Against Euthanasia and Physician-Assisted Suicide.* Montreal: McGill-Queen's University Press, 2002.
Ian Stevenson	*Where Reincarnation and Biology Intersect.* Westport, CT: Praeger, 1997.
Michael M. Uhlmann, ed.	*Last Rights? Assisted Suicide and Euthanasia Debated.* Washington, DC: Ethics and Public Policy Center, 1998.
Brian de Vries, ed.	*End of Life Issues: Interdisciplinary and Multidimensional Perspectives.* New York: Springer, 1999.
Marilyn Webb	*The Good Death: The New American Search to Reshape the End of Life.* New York: Bantam Books, 1997.
Sue Woodman	*Last Rights: The Struggle over the Right to Die.* New York: Plenum Trade, 1998.
Brian Wowk	*Cryonics: Reaching for Tomorrow.* Scottsdale, AZ: Alcor Life Extension Foundation, 1993.
Stuart J. Younger, Robert M. Arnold, and Renie Shapiro, eds.	*The Definition of Death: Contemporary Controversies.* Baltimore, MD: Johns Hopkins University Press, 1999.
Steven J. Zeitlin and Ilana Beth Harlow	*Giving a Voice to Sorrow: Personal Responses to Death and Mourning.* New York: Perigee Books, 2001.
Marjorie Zucker, ed.	*The Right to Die Debate: A Documentary History.* Westport, CT: Greenwood Press, 1999.

Index